CONFLICT RESOLUTION:
NEW APPROACHES AND METHOD

Conflict resolution: new approaches and methods

Peace and Conflict Issues
UNESCO PUBLISHING

Published in 2000 by the United Nations Educational,
Scientific and Cultural Organization,
7 place de Fontenoy, 75352 Paris 07 SP, France

Composed by Gérard Prosper
Printed by Imprimerie Blanchard,
92350 Le Plessis-Robinson

ISBN 92-3-103640-8

Preface

The present volume in the UNESCO series entitled 'Peace and Conflict Issues' is devoted to conflict resolution. The subject matter, identified in consultation with the members of the Advisory Board for this series,* deals with the theme in its various dimensions and brings together research results and reflections of scholars.

In a world where many areas are afflicted with internal and international conflicts, making peace a tangible reality is of critical importance. Preventive measures, peace-making as well as post-conflict peace-building, pose enormous challenges and call for action to eliminate sources of conflict and violence. The international community must address the political, economic and cultural factors that lead to conflicts.

Peace-keeping and peace-building have become multifunctional objectives. Peace-keeping should facilitate the political process of building confidence, finding negotiated solutions to long-standing differences and fostering democratic approaches to the resolution of internal conflicts. It is also a means of promoting a dialogue of cultures and cultural pluralism.

Within the United Nations system, action is being mobilized in the search for the peaceful resolution of conflicts. Specialized Agencies and, in particular, regional organizations are participating actively in this endeavour. An important role is

---

*   A list of the Board members can be found at the end of this volume.

also played by the International Court of Justice as well as by arbitration and mediation procedures. During the reconstruction period following the conclusion of a peace agreement, vast fields for action open up, especially the building of civil peace based on respect for human rights and the ideals of democracy. These necessitate a range of activities. UNESCO contributes to them by helping, through its national programmes for a culture of peace, to lay the foundations for reconciliation between the parties to a conflict and by exploring and assuming new roles in order to carry out its ethical mission – constructing peace in the minds of men and women. The Organization seeks to be a catalyser and the centre of joint efforts and concerted action at international, regional and national levels.

The present volume provides insight into new conditions for security and the promotion of innovative methods of conflict resolution. It should be be useful to specialized centres, academic institutions, educators and researchers working on the theme of peace and conflict. It may also be of interest to all UNESCO partners: governments, national commissions, parliamentarians, religious leaders, non-governmental organizations and the mass media. By provoking further reflections on the vital question of innovative approaches to peaceful conflict resolution and management, this publication will, we hope, contribute to the endeavours of the international community to consolidate peace.

The Year 2000 has been proclaimed as the International Year for the Culture of Peace by the United Nations General Assembly. This volume can be seen as a modest contribution to the ongoing reflection on how to limit and eliminate violence in internal and international life, and how to build a culture of peace within and between states.

Contents

The contribution of the International Court of Justice towards keeping and restoring peace

Mohammed Bedjaoui

The ambitions of the authors of the United Nations Charter were totally different from the ambitions of those who drafted the Covenant of the League of Nations. They were no longer content to seek a peace which would simply preserve a precarious status quo. What they were aiming at was an entirely new kind of international society, which would gradually acquire more progress, justice, equality and fellowship, which would be both more integrated and more universal, and whose members would work actively and jointly towards a complete and lasting peace – energetically and efficiently managed.

Let us first take a quick look at the relevant articles of the Charter.

Article 2, paragraph 4, of the Charter is widely known: the Members of the Organization shall refrain from the use of force in any manner inconsistent with the purposes of the United Nations. Here we have the specific declaration of a wider principle which would thereafter be sanctioned by customary international law.

Article 33 of the Charter makes it compulsory for states who are parties to any dispute to 'first of all, seek a solution by negotiation, enquiry, mediation, conciliation, arbitration, judicial settlement, . . . or other peaceful means of their own choice'.

From the combination of Articles 2 and 33 of the Charter, we can draw the constructive conclusion that the Charter makes the pacific settlement of disputes an official obligation.

States must therefore settle their disputes by peaceful means and they must exercise good faith in choosing the type of mechanism that they consider the best adapted to solving the conflict that opposes them. This prerequisite of good faith, stipulated in paragraph 2 of Article 2 of the Charter, is important. States may choose the peaceful means of settling their disputes, but they are obliged to choose one from those available. Once this means of settlement has been chosen, they must seek in good faith a solution to their conflict.

Article 33 of the Charter therefore leaves the choice open for peaceful means to be used either within or outside the framework of the Organization. Concerning the Organization, there is no indication of the roles that certain bodies are more specifically called upon to play in this respect. Such indications must be sought in other chapters of the Charter, and especially in those devoted to each of the organs concerned. Article 33 makes specific mention of 'judicial settlement', and Article 36, paragraph 3, stipulates that when the Security Council makes recommendations for this kind of settlement, '[it] should also take into consideration that legal disputes should as a general rule be referred by the parties to the International Court of Justice in accordance with the provisions of the Statute of the Court'.

Article 7 of the Charter designates the Court as a principal organ of the United Nations system, and Article 92 designates it as the Organization's principal judicial body. What must be remembered at this stage is that there is no provision, either in the Charter or in the Statute of the Court, limiting the Court's action in the exercise of its roles. Given this fact, the Court appears to be an essential part, not only of the machinery defined in the Charter for the pacific settlement of disputes, but also of the general system which the Charter has established for maintaining peace and international security, of which the Court is the essential complement.

However, the Court's action in this field has limits inherent in its very nature. The Court cannot obviously investigate a dispute of its own accord, as can or must, according to the case, the Security Council.

This is the major difference between these two principal organs. States remain extremely reticent about the idea of submitting to compulsory jurisdiction without their specific consent. The principle of consent is still the basic rule in this

The contribution of
the International Court
of Justice towards keeping
and restoring peace

11

field. There is as yet no international jurisdiction with compulsory and universal application. There is, admittedly, a legal obligation to use peaceful means to settle disputes, especially as the Charter has banned the use of force. But settlement by means specifically judicial is not imposed at the outset without the consent of the state, which can choose a means of pacific settlement other than judicial among those mentioned in Article 33 of the Charter.

International public opinion does not usually understand why the International Court of Justice does not of its own accord arbitrate in all disputes between states, and especially in those which degenerate into armed conflict. The reply is that international justice is still based on consent, which defines the structural limits of the contribution which the Court can make to maintaining peace and international security.

However, once an application is made, the Court fully plays the distinguished role entrusted to it by the Charter. Its jurisprudence shows quite clearly the determining role that it has played on various occasions, not only in settling numerous disputes, but also, directly, in keeping or restoring the peace between parties. In this respect, several types of contribution can be highlighted.

Firstly, there are cases where the Court's decision itself on the merits of a case puts an immediate and permanent stop to a dispute which has sometimes been threatening the peace for many years, and where other means of peaceful solution have proved ineffectual (for example: frontier dispute between Burkina Faso and Mali; island frontier dispute between El Salvador and Honduras, territorial dispute between the Libyan Arab Jamahiriya and Chad). There are other, less spectacular cases where the Court's decision, either on the merits of a case (for example: fisheries jurisdiction; military and paramilitary activities in and against Nicaragua) or even, at a preliminary stage, on its jurisdiction (for example: border and transborder armed actions (Nicaragua versus Honduras)), while at first finding no favour with either party, has finally weighed considerably in the successful outcome of out-of-court negotiations between them.

But on yet other occasions, the Court's action is a determining factor in keeping or restoring peace between parties before it has even had time to make a ruling. In this respect, certain cases where provisional measures have been indicated have proved particularly successful.

Allow me to recall – as it is perhaps less known – the order of 10 January 1986 indicating provisional measures, which was made by the Chamber of which I was President and which examined the frontier dispute between Burkina Faso and Mali. This order was delivered at a public meeting on the very next day to that on which the judge heard the parties, at a time when serious incidents had occurred between their respective armed forces. It is in many ways exemplary. In it, the Court stresses:

(1)   that when two states decide to refer a case to the Court, and when incidents occur which involve the use of force, there is no doubt whatsoever that it is in the Court's power and that it is its duty to indicate provisional measures where and as necessary;

(2)   that states are always free to negotiate or settle certain aspects of a dispute submitted to the Court in other ways; but

(3)   that the Court cannot be deprived of the rights and duties which are its own in the case of the matter being referred to another organ by the parties;

(4)   that Article 41 of the Statute obliges the Court itself to seek and to indicate the provisional measures which must be taken; and finally,

(5)   that the Court must indicate provisional measures with a view to the parties ensuring that they avoid any act which might aggravate or spread the dispute, while respecting the cease-fire which has been established and withdrawing their armed forces to positions to be determined.

This order had almost immediate effect, while negotiations continued within the framework of other, mainly regional organizations.

Sometimes the mere submission of a case to the Court can have an immediate defusing effect, thus circumscribing and 'containing' the dispute by preventing it from degenerating (e.g., The Corfu Channel Case). The mere act of referral can also hasten an amicable arrangement between parties, which results in the case being withdrawn (e.g., Pakistani prisoners of war). In other cases, referral brings about a unilateral change of attitude on the part of the defendant, thus removing the object of the claimant's action (e.g., nuclear trials).

All this is valid for the rulings of the Court. But we must not forget the major impact that the Court's advisory function can have on peace-keeping, whether directly or indirectly. This advice makes a considerable contribution, not only to

The contribution of 13
the International Court
of Justice towards keeping
and restoring peace

the smooth running of international organizations, but also to the advancement of law and legal discipline. Indeed, we must not lose sight of the fact that a relevant legal question, asked of the Court at the right moment, can, either by the reply it receives or simply in itself, prove to be an effective instrument for preventive diplomacy or make a substantial contribution to the solution of a dispute that has already arisen. There is no doubt that there are many ways in which the advisory procedure, used in the absence of any immediate conflict, constitutes a privileged means for the Court to prevent and defuse tensions by stating the law. There are numerous cases in the past where advisory opinions have had a considerable diplomatic and political effect (e.g., the various opinions of the Court on South West Africa (Namibia)).

Many opinions have also had a determining effect on progress in international law since the end of the Second World War. Allow me simply to mention as an example the opinion – which was revolutionary in the legal world at the time – that the Court gave as early as 1949 on the objective international personality of the Organization and its capacity to demand reparation.

The International Court of Justice is thus an important part of the overall system instituted by the Charter for settling disputes peacefully and keeping the peace. And, in carrying out its responsibilities to the full, the Court plays a distinguished role to this end. It does this in various ways, but always within the limits of the powers that the international community decided to confer upon it at a given moment of its existence, in line with the perception that the same community then had of its duties. So, we might ask, in spite of all this: Why does the Court appear too often to be out of step with reality? Why are certain, particularly serious disputes not referred to it, when these call for a speedy, fair and lasting solution, and when a judicial settlement could defuse the situation perfectly?

I shall not dwell on the impossibility for the Court to take on a conflict of its own accord, since, as I have already mentioned, international justice is based on states' consent. I should like, therefore, to add other replies to the question I have just asked. First of all, it must be stated that for some time now there has been a marked and growing renewal of interest in the Court's jurisdiction. In June 1999, the Court had nineteen cases pending, which represent a volume of activity that it has never known in the past. At the same time, the Court's jurisdiction is constantly spreading: new declarations are being deposited recognizing its compulsory nature; new arbitration clauses are being inserted into treaties; and many reservations to such clauses are regularly withdrawn. All this is indeed encouraging, but it obviously does not reply to the question asked.

I must in fact stress that a quick comparison between the present Court's volume of activity and that of its predecessor is somewhat disappointing. I shall simply point out, purely for information, that the former Permanent Court took no less than fifty-eight decisions (rulings and advisory opinions combined) in nineteen years (between 1922 and 1940), meaning an average of three decisions per year. Over fifty-three years (between 1946 and mid-1999), the present Court has delivered a total of sixty-eight judgements and twenty-four advisory opinions, which represents an average of less than two decisions per year. It is true that the intense activity of the Permanent Court was largely due to the special responsibilities conferred upon it by the peace treaties relating to the overall settlement following the First World War. But a more detailed comparison can be made. The old Permanent Court would appear, in a way, to have been more present in the minds of the states at that time. It should thus be noted that, of the forty-eight states parties to the Statute of the Court in January 1939, thirty-six had made declarations recognizing its compulsory jurisdiction. The current ratio is much lower, since to date, of 187 states parties to the Court's Statute, there are only sixty-two declarations in force recognizing the compulsory jurisdiction of the Court.

Despite the various reasons that could be found for this, it must be admitted that the situation seems singularly paradoxical when we consider the role which each of the two Courts was called upon to play in its own legal and institutional environment. Indeed, the International Court of Justice, which in San Francisco was specifically intended to become an institution officially distinct from its predecessor, and fully integrated with the new organization and its founding concerns and objectives, could have been expected from the outset to be associated much more closely and significantly than the old Court with world problems. In fact, this has not only not been the case in the past, but the situation appears to persist in many ways today.

The contribution of   15
the International Court
of Justice towards keeping
and restoring peace

So this brings me back to the question I asked a little earlier, about why the Court, finally, cannot make full use of the powers that it holds from the Charter or of its peace-making talents in the sorely troubled international relations of today's world, as we begin a new century. Various attempts have been made to reply to this question, which all have their interest, but also their limits.

At one time, certain observers believed that there was some hostility on the part of given groups of states towards an institution that appeared to them as belonging too exclusively to a given legal and cultural system. Today, this explanation is largely belied by the facts. Since 1946, the Court has had referred to it matters concerning all the continents and implicating states belonging to varied legal systems. The almost universal composition of the Court which, according to Article 9 of its Statute, must ensure fair representation of the main forms of civilization and of the principal legal systems of the world, combined with its working methods, and in particular its collegial nature, are solid guarantees of a perfect understanding of the concerns of all states. The Court is composed of magistrates who are equal, independent and impartial. At the Court there is neither the right to veto nor political patronage. The Court delivers a legal verdict, following an extremely meticulous examination of each case, without ignoring meta-legal elements or overlooking the parties' aspirations, but never losing sight of the essentials, which are justice and peace. There are many smaller or weaker states that have obtained from the Court what they doubtless could never have obtained elsewhere.

Other observers have tried to categorize the Court's field of activity by making a typological breakdown of its jurisdiction on the basis of past cases. They have come to the premature conclusion that the Court is incompetent to examine disputes other than those traditionally referred to it. It would thus appear that there is a sort of Court 'preserve', of which the Court itself is prisoner. Not only does this interpretation have no basis in the texts, but it is also too limited to explain why many concrete disputes, which should come within this 'preserve' (for example frontier disputes) have never been – and indeed never will be – submitted to the Court.

A number of complaints traditionally made by certain governments concerning the Court have been suggested to explain their reticence to use it. One of these complaints is the alleged slowness of the proceedings. It is true that, on average, the Court takes three to five years to settle a case. This is, I admit, a long time, although such delays seem to be quite usual in domestic legal systems, which should a priori be better equipped for cases to be dealt with as promptly as necessary. I shall simply mention that the Court, which is very aware of the problem, undertook a revision of various provisions in its Rules as early as 1972 with a view to putting the situation as much as possible to rights. But there are limits to what the Court can do when the sovereign states which submit important cases wish – and who can blame them? – to give themselves the best possible chance of success by asking to be allowed to file additional pleadings and documents, or to have sufficient time to present their arguments, first in writing, then orally. In fact, when the Court is at last able to deliberate, things usually move very quickly, since there are usually only a few months – or sometimes only a few weeks – between the end of the oral proceedings and the delivery of the Court's decision. The speed will certainly be remembered with which the Court, at the request of the General Assembly, gave an advisory opinion on the question concerning the Applicability of the Obligation to Arbitrate under Section 21 of the United Nations Headquarters Agreement of 26 June 1947. For this case, the public hearing ended on 12 April 1988, and the Court's opinion – despite its being quite long and complex – was given only fourteen days later, on 26 April 1988. The early dispatch of cases, which is one of the basic conditions of sound administration and justice, therefore depends mainly on the determination, not of the Court, but of those who come before it.

The second complaint to which I referred concerns the financial costs of submitting a case to the Court. For the Organization's Member States, which contribute to the budget, access to the Court is free. The absence of costs for the proceedings themselves does not, of course, mean that the exercise is cost-free. Parties have to bear various costs, and notably advocates' fees, which can prove to be quite substantial. The cornerstone of any legal proceedings is the fundamental principle of equality between parties, and this is the principle underlying all the arrangements for proceedings contained in the Statute and Rules of the Court. We all understand, however, that this 'official' equality, capital though it may be, is not sufficient to calm the worries of the less advantaged states. True justice means

The contribution of 17
the International Court
of Justice towards keeping
and restoring peace

everyone being equal before the judge, not only according to the law, but in reality. It is for this reason that I paid a special tribute before the United Nations General Assembly to the Secretary-General's remarkable initiative, which led to the creation, in 1989, of a special fund to assist Member States which were unable to bear the costs incurred by the submission of a dispute to the Court. Such judicial solidarity, if the system were to be confirmed and enlarged, would without doubt be a sign of great maturity in the international community.

None of the explanations, then, appear to reply satisfactorily to my earlier question. I shall, then, attempt my own modest explanation. This is by no means meant to be the definitive answer, but will, I hope, prompt us to think along new lines. I have the impression that when answers are sought to the question, insufficient attention is attached to what I would quite simply call the 'psychology of states'. And yet this 'psychology' seems to have been subject, with the passing of time, to the growing impact of various attempts to 'categorize' reality. These can have harmful effects when they cease to be an exercise in understanding and turn into basic assumptions. I refer particularly here to the famous notions of what constitutes a 'legal' dispute and what constitutes a 'political' dispute.

Admittedly, as specified by Article 38 of the Statute, the mission of the Court, as a legal organ, is 'to decide in accordance with international law such disputes as are submitted to it'. As it has to make legal judgements, the Court can only examine questions framed in legal terms. The implications of this irrefutable fact have nevertheless long been subject to misinterpretation. Under the influence, no doubt, of ideas inherited from an epoch preceding the adoption of the Charter, states seemed for many years to feel that the only disputes that could be submitted to the Court were those believed to be solely judicial, and which were in fact perceived as being relatively marginal or minor. Governments did not seem to realize that the Court might usefully be apprised of the judicial aspects of a dispute with a nevertheless significant political component. Fortunately the fiction which nurtured the 'legal versus political disputes' dichotomy is now almost completely discredited. Indeed, it is no longer contested that the very existence of a dispute, whatever it may be, must have a political dimension, and that there are very few disputes, however politically important they may be, which do not have a legal dimension. There is room, therefore, for optimism, in hoping that states, taking inspiration from this approach – which is both infinitely more realistic and respectful of the complexity of international relations – will review their criteria for applying to the Court and will never at any time forget that application to the Court, even when this only concerns a subsidiary legal aspect of a much broader dispute, can, as I have already stressed, have an immediate defusing effect and transform the physiognomy of the dispute. This is because the decision of the Court in itself is also, in each case, the consequence of a political choice, which is itself motivated, according to events, by shifting factors which might be diplomatic, economic, historical, political or even psychological. This is why, in the past, a number of disputes traditionally recognized as referable to the Court have not been submitted.

The Court's credibility as the principal organ and distinguished means for the pacific settlement of disputes is therefore mainly in the hands of states. I am deeply convinced that it will only be when the members of the international community rid themselves of old prejudices and are – dare I say? – psychologically ready to apply just as naturally to the Court as to the political organs, without considering this act to be necessarily more serious, litigious or hostile, that it will be able to carry out its mission to the full. Perhaps certain states tend to fear judicial settlement for the double reason that, contrary to a political settlement, it would, firstly, totally escape their grasp and that, secondly, bearing in mind the assumed rigidity of the law, it would tend always to be less favourable to them. These fears are mainly unfounded. I repeat that application to the Court does not prevent continued negotiations between parties, nor referral to other organs. On the contrary, as we have seen from many recent examples, submission of a dispute, or of one aspect of a dispute, to the Court obliges the parties to frame their grievances in objective terms, and thus has the effect of defusing the situation between them, sometimes prompting them to renew discussions. It can even, ultimately, lead to an amicable out-of-court arrangement.

On the other hand, it is clearly a mistake to think that strict application of the law invariably leads to the establishment of the arguments of one of the parties and to the rejection of those of the other, as if there always had to be a 'winner' and a 'loser'. Apart from the fact that there cannot be a 'loser' when a dispute is settled serenely and when peace prevails, it must be stressed that the Court –

The contribution of   19
the International Court
of Justice towards keeping
and restoring peace

because of the nature of the law which it applies and the role which it plays – is sure never to apply the law blindly. And this quality is to be found more certainly in the Court than in any other judicial institution. While international law is sufficiently clear and precise to provide the parties with all the legal security to which they legitimately aspire, it remains by its nature – need I say it? – both flexible and open. The Court itself has in fact explained on several occasions that it considers that its making legal judgements in no way excludes – quite the contrary – taking into account *infra legem* equity, meaning that form of equity that constitutes a method of interpreting the law and is one of its qualities. We know that there are specific areas of international law, such as the law of the sea, where there are constant references to principles of equity. As an integral part of the peace-keeping system established by the Charter, the Court never loses sight of this final objective and always does its utmost to apply the law in the manner most likely to achieve it.

While we observe that the Court is not used as well as it should be for litigation, and we are not only speaking of quantity but also, above all, of quality, this also applies to the advisory proceedings.

The advisory channel is perhaps even less well used than the litigation channel, especially when we take into account the constant advantages that this system offers to the international organizations, its flexible implementation and the fact that it is essentially non-restrictive. It is very probable that the sometimes inaccurate image that states have of the Court's role has spread to the organizations of which they are members, as these organizations are prey to the same ambiguities and, in fact, are imbued with the same reservations. I am ready to wager that a truer understanding on the part of the members of the international community, both of the nature of the mission conferred upon the Court and of the potential that its advisory role represents, would soon result in increased applications to such proceedings, which are indeed essential if the entire community is gradually to integrate the law.

The immediate priority is, therefore, in my view, for governments to show the political will to take a fresh, more realistic view of the Court. This is the price, which seems small enough to me, that must be paid if the Court is to recover the place in world affairs intended for it by the authors of the Charter.

In the longer term, the Court's fate will of course be linked to that of the United Nations Organization and, particularly, to the latter's ability to adapt speedily and efficiently to the spectacular upheavals that have left their mark on international relations as we near the end of the century.

Thought is already being given to this matter. It goes without saying that any studies on the question must include the way in which the Court operates. States, traditionally considered as basic and necessary to the international legal order, are alone at present in having access to litigation by the Court. However, they are no longer, as they were in the 1920s, the sole players in international relations, nor the sole interlocutors in keeping the peace. Day after day, international relations show us that it is increasingly necessary to take account of other infra- or supra-state bodies. In the same way, access to advisory proceedings will need to be opened up if we consider the enormous potential that these proceedings represent. The possibility of applying to the Court for advisory opinions could be envisaged, not only for the other organs of the Organization – and particularly the Secretary-General – but also, where necessary, for other organizations which are not part of the United Nations system, but whose contribution to keeping the peace, on the regional level, for example, is significant. These questions are of major importance for the future of the Court and for world peace, and call for very careful examination in the near future.

An Agenda for Peace as a new means of settling conflicts

Yves Daudet

In recent years, UNESCO has launched a work programme and wide-ranging interdisciplinary reflection, with the purpose of creating a 'culture of peace'. This programme has received the support of the United Nations General Assembly, notably in its resolution 51/101 of 12 December 1996. And the time is indeed ripe for such an undertaking, when we consider the new world geopolitical situation as we start a new century, and the erratic course of recent history, which has resulted in conflicts not always being settled under the conditions or according to the mechanisms of the United Nations Charter since it was signed in 1945. The political situation caused by antagonism between the two blocs practically brought the Security Council to a standstill and resulted in recourse to substitute measures such as the Acheson resolution (377-V). The same situation made it impossible to implement the military enforcement system under Chapter VII (with the result that it has been difficult to turn the fine ideal of collective security into reality), and resulted in the invention of the United Nations troops and the peace-keeping operations, which correspond to a different philosophy, though the goal to serve peace is still the same.

Of course, it can be deplored that certain mechanisms, finalized with such care in the Charter, have never even seen the light of day, or are only partially applied in conditions differing from those originally envisaged. When all is considered, the situation is not surprising. The United Nations is a political organization with extremely broad and ambitious aims. It is therefore quite normal that world politics should effect changes in perspectives, bringing the need for new formulae better adapted to the needs and realities of worldwide society without, necessarily, implying changes to the Charter. In this respect, a brief glance at the fifty or so years that have passed since the Charter came into force reveals how fertile this period has been in major events. It has been necessary to heal the wounds caused by conflicts which, as recalled by the preamble to the Charter, had 'brought untold sorrow to mankind', to rebuild regions devastated by war, and to set up a mechanism to protect human rights and ensure that what Bertold Brecht called the 'unspeakable monster' never again raises its head. Decolonization has also had to be organized, under-development tackled, and the shock of the Cold War absorbed, including the subsequent end of this with the collapse of the whole Communist bloc. Finally, the United Nations system has had to be made to work despite the fact that its members have more than tripled, and that it now has to face up to conflicts of a new kind, more often internal than international, and to more varied breaches of peace than those envisaged in 1945.

With about 280 vetoes blocking its action since the creation of the United Nations, it was only in 1990, with the end of the Cold War, that the Security Council was finally able to carry out its mission under the Charter, and to become the main instrument for preventing and settling conflicts and keeping the peace. For the first time in its history, on 31 January 1992, the Security Council met at the level of heads of states and governments, and invited the Secretary-General to prepare 'his analysis and recommendations on ways of strengthening and making more efficient within the framework and provisions of the Charter the capacity of the United Nations for preventive diplomacy, for peacemaking and for peace-keeping'. This study, entitled *An Agenda for Peace* (A/47/277–S/24111 of 31/1/1992), followed in 1995 by a *Supplement to an Agenda for Peace* (A/50/60–S/1995/1 of 3/1/1995) consisting of a position paper on the occasion of the fiftieth anniversary of the United Nations, starts out with a rather conventional concept of peace and the means that can be used to ensure it in a world that has just experienced fundamental changes and profound upheavals. In fact, as we shall see later, the Secretary-General finally goes far beyond this concept by proposing quite a new concept of peace, and therefore of United Nations action. However, before we

An Agenda for Peace
as a new means
of settling conflicts   23

come to these innovations, the Agenda appears at first glance to be a sort of inventory of the international community perceived through the changing boundaries and new structures that are taking shape, and which should give the Charter a new vitality and a second wind.

Transcending all the upheavals and changing boundaries, as well as the globalization that is creeping up on us imperceptibly, while already infringing, in fact, the notion of frontier, one basic element remains: the state in its sovereignty, right at the centre of the international apparatus, despite prophecies announcing its demise (no one, however, seems capable of predicting what would replace it). The Secretary-General states that 'the foundation stone' of the international community 'is and must remain the state', thus using the traditional and established principles of international law as the basis for his argument. Sovereignty and territorial integrity are still the best guarantees for stability. It is impossible to imagine that peace could be preserved in the event of ethnic, religious, political or other groups breaking off into so many individual bodies. However, it is the responsibility of states to find the right formulae to ensure that such groups living on their territory possess a status guaranteeing their legitimate rights. Without this, peace cannot be ensured, whether within the state or without, because of the interdependency and ties often existing between communities beyond state frontiers. Peace in these circumstances is heavily dependent on the respect of human rights and the general application of democratic principles.

The transformations in Eastern Europe, with the break-up of the USSR and the collapse of Yugoslavia, are good illustrations of these patterns. They have effectively given rise to the appearance on the international scene of new states which, in the opinion of the Secretary-General, present certain similarities to decolonized states, since they also have freed themselves from a yoke. While the cohesion of these new states is threatened by internal conflicts that rock their foundations, and by the ethnic, religious, social or other struggles that affect them, they none the less remain sovereign states. However, the difficulties of which they are the primary victims engender insecurity which is more global and which affects the international community. In a world become interdependent, it is indeed frequent for the domestic situation of one state to spread to neighbouring states and to have repercussions on the whole region, or even beyond. It is for this reason that the Secretary-General took care to stress that the concept of international security was not easy to grasp, and could undergo contradictory developments. Thus, nuclear weapons, long considered to be the major risk, have occasioned agreements between the principal nuclear powers. Meanwhile, the proliferation of weapons of widespread destruction and of conventional arms makes international security extremely uncertain. Apartheid has been dismantled, but other kinds of ethnic tension appear, and acts of genocide are perpetrated. Advances in technology and in communications do represent progress, but they create new risks of ecological damage, disruption to family and community, or even growing disparities between rich and poor. In short, these evils, which are multiple and varied, are sources – but can also be consequences – of conflicts.

In the end, it is peace itself that has undergone a profound change. The supple notion of peace as conceived by the United Nations has made it possible to add on very different elements to adapt to the concerns of a given point in time. Following a natural order, and using a very open and flexible interpretation of the word 'peace', the United Nations first undertook to restore international peace in the conventional sense. It then went on to seek the liberation of enslaved peoples – something that was not foreseen in the wording of the Charter – and then to set up mechanisms for economic assistance in order to ensure peace through development, in the hope of a new world economic order.

At present, by continuing in this way to give 'new names' to peace (just as Pope Paul VI did to Third World development) the United Nations goes so far as to assist democracy through state-restoring operations.

In doing so, the United Nations could seem to be encroaching upon the state's prerogative with regard to domestic matters. It is true that the term 'peace-keeping operations of the second generation', which is used to designate them, underlines quite clearly their attachment to the general aims of Article 1 of the Charter. Nevertheless, the United Nations is also attentive to Article 2 paragraph 7 and to the principle of non-intervention in domestic matters when the actual purpose of the operation concerned touches directly upon aspects of state sovereignty such as the form or designation of government, etc. But this gradual shift of the Organization towards a purpose which until recently has been more

An Agenda for Peace
as a new means
of settling conflicts

25

or less foreign to it does not represent an aim to interfere in domestic matters as such; it is simply the direct consequence of the search for peace in the new context of international relations. Indeed, at present, there is less concern over collective security than over the many internal conflicts, with the obvious risk which they always comprise, and which often materializes, of their spreading internationally. And it is true that a conflict which a few years ago would have been ascribed to East–West rivalry, often originates in a society that has fallen apart, or in the ravages caused by a dictatorship, or is due to social unrest caused by a lack of democracy. In consequence, international and internal aspects often become mixed, and assistance for rebuilding the state, which is an internal affair, becomes part of peace-keeping and peace-building, which are international affairs. Moreover, it is clear that the distinction is always difficult to make in this area between what is internal and what is international. Indeed, the United Nations frequently stresses that such or such a domestic situation is creating disorders and breaches of security in a given region, thus legitimizing its actions in the service of peace.

In drafting *An Agenda for Peace* and its *Supplement,* the Secretary-General took into consideration these major world trends and was guided by his desire to develop the United Nations' capacity to reply both to the needs of the international community and to its expectations, following the Organization's very real upward turn at the end of the 1980s. These two texts, which concern peace taken both in the conventional and modern sense of the word, were then complemented by *An Agenda for Development* (A/48/935 of 6/5/1995) and *An Agenda for Democratization* (A/51/761 of 20/12/1996). These texts, covering the various aspects of peace mentioned above, provide us with a triptych forming the United Nations doctrine for peace at the dawning of the new millennium.

This doctrine confirms what has been achieved in the safeguard of peace while opening new channels for a more global notion of peace, to the extent that, in certain respects, new United Nations operations for settling conflicts usually involve a technical-assistance component.

By this globalized notion of peace, and the perspectives given in *An Agenda for Peace* taken in the context of the three mutually complementary agendas, the Secretary-General makes an undoubtedly major contribution to the resolution of conflicts in today's world. On the whole, this was extremely well received both by individual Member States and the political bodies of the United Nations – the General Assembly and Security Council. The Security Council did however avoid taking a decision on certain aspects (early warning, reactivation of Article 43 and following Articles of the Charter, see below), expressing the reservations of certain permanent members.

The doctrinal thinking underlying the Agenda is constantly aware of practical considerations and constraints. It relies on the letter and spirit of the Charter and its various amendments as instruments for peace in their own right. The Agenda is an analysis, therefore, of the established mechanisms for settling conflicts which need, however, to be adapted to the realities of today's world in order to restore peace. But it goes much further. The world has changed, not simply due to the end of the Cold War, but also because of the globalization of recent years, and the new actors in international relations, non-governmental organizations, private bodies, etc. The result is that frontiers between states, while they still exist, are somewhat porous. Domestic and international affairs are no longer strictly compartmentalized; on the contrary, they interpenetrate and have a mutual influence on each other. This being the case, the notion of peace spreads to new areas, and becomes a broader, more complex notion, rich in different elements, which together contribute to its lasting nature. The programme contained in the Agendas also aims at strengthening peace.

RESTORING PEACE

This is the United Nations' first mission, and the one which, above all others, justifies its creation and appears at the top of the list of the Organization's aims. The Charter concentrated above all on mechanisms for settling disputes peaceably and on coercive action which could be taken in the case of a breach of the peace.

In 1945, therefore, future events were envisaged within a certain historical context, and differed essentially in their degrees of acuteness. This context underwent a total upheaval with the Cold War, followed by another in the 1990s which made it necessary to reconsider the entire system of the Charter and its amendments.

An Agenda for Peace 27
as a new means
of settling conflicts

Chapter VI of the Charter

Concerning the elements relating to Chapter VI, the Agenda also refers to the means detailed in the *Manila Declaration on the Peaceful Settlement of International Disputes* (37/10 of 15/11/1982) or in the *Declaration on the Prevention and Removal of Disputes and Situations which May Threaten International Peace and Security and on the Role of the United Nations in this Field* (43/51 of 5/12/1988) or lastly in resolution 44/21 of 15/11/1989 on *Enhancing International Peace, Security and International Co-operation in All Its Aspects in accordance with the Charter of the United Nations.* Possibilities are ample, therefore, and of a nature to cover all possible hypotheses. If, despite these various instruments, it has been impossible to solve numerous conflicts, the responsibility does not lie with the United Nations, but with the lack of willingness of the parties involved. Indeed, it is important to stress once again that, in spite of its judicial character, the United Nations does not have a real will of its own. The United Nations is the mirror of the wishes of its Member States, and acts on the condition that the states accept this representation and within the limits which they assign to the Organization. Thus, the Articles of the Charter and the very many legal acts which have since been adopted mean nothing if there is no political will on the part of states to bring them to life. The word 'states' here is used to cover not only those directly involved in the conflict, but also all those that make up the international community as a whole. Indeed, how many conflicts remain unresolved, not so much because of the attitude of the states directly concerned as due to the indifference of the international community to events occurring in poor and little-heard-of regions, far from the geopolitical and strategic hubs that interest the major powers? In such a case, it usually takes a massive violation of human rights and public awareness within Member States, which depends mainly on the role the media decide to play, for international action to be undertaken. The United Nations in itself has, therefore, little control over these facts of life. In the Agenda, the Secretary-General can only invite states to make better and more use of the rules and institutions available to them.

In the current political context, certain organs are more operational than they were formerly. Such, naturally and most important of all, is the case of the Security Council, where 'with greater unity has come leverage and persuasive power to lead hostile parties towards negotiations'. As a consequence, the Security Council is now able to take advantage of the Charter's entire range of measures. The more favourable context also allows the Secretary-General to play a more active role, particularly by offering to act as mediator, either at the request of the General Assembly or the Security Council or, perhaps with more effect, spontaneously. Finally, the Secretary-General's appeal for the International Court of Justice to be more widely used has been heard, since its schedule nowadays is always overloaded. Nevertheless, the exhortations on this point in the Agenda are not always realistic. In particular, it is not certain that much progress has been made regarding acceptance of the compulsory jurisdiction of the Court based on Article 36, paragraph 2, of its Statute, and it is to be feared that the Secretary-General's wish on this point will remain just that. As for the suggestion that wider use be made of Chambers jurisdiction, this will depend on the wishes of the states.

Independently of these different measures under Chapter VI for the peaceful settlement of disputes, the Charter also includes recourse to coercion, when this seems necessary to restore peace, under Chapter VII.

Chapter VII of the Charter

With regard to Chapter VII, the Agenda is an opportunity to consider coercive measures in the light of past experience and of new world geopolitics.

Over recent years, economic sanctions have been used on several occasions in application of Article 41 of the Charter. In the *Supplement to an Agenda to Peace* (paragraphs 66 et seq.) the Secretary-General rightly deems it necessary to recall the purpose of sanctions. Their purpose is to exert pressure on a state in order to bring it to modify behaviour that is threatening international peace and security. The aim is not to punish or otherwise exact retribution. The Security Council is a political not a judicial organ, and it is important to avoid giving the impression that there has been a shift in the purposes of sanctions. And yet the difficulty involved in taking a decision to lift or continue sanctions can have the effect of giving this impression. It is also important not to neglect the moral aspects of sanctions, which automatically lead us to question the legitimacy of a mechanism that results in suffering for the population without necessarily changing the position of political leaders. These considerations do not aim to call the use of

An Agenda for Peace 29
as a new means
of settling conflicts

sanctions into question. They do however underline the necessity of finding appropriate corrective measures in the form of humanitarian assistance to vulnerable groups.

Attention must also be paid to the unpleasant consequences and particular damage suffered by certain states (for example, states neighbouring the target state or having a large volume of trade with it, so that the embargo against the target state destabilizes their own economies). This possibility is covered in Article 50 of the Charter. As a rule, however, such situations have not been settled satisfactorily. It is for this reason that the Agenda draws the attention of the Security Council, in the name of equity, to the need for measures to assist states suffering damage in these circumstances. This would, moreover, be in the general interests of the system of sanctions and its smooth running. It is obvious, indeed, that if adequate compensation is not found for states suffering 'on the rebound', they will quite simply be tempted not to apply the sanctions. The Secretary-General's voice has also been heard on this point as, in the case of the conflicts in the former Yugoslavia, a vast reflection was undertaken and measures were taken in favour of certain states who had claimed the benefit of Article 50 upon the Security Council's adopting economic sanctions against Serbia.

Concretely, in paragraph 75 of the *Supplement to an Agenda for Peace,* the Secretary-General proposes the setting up of a mechanism to carry out five functions in the area of sanctions: (i) to assess, before sanctions are imposed, their political impact on the target country and on third countries; (ii) to monitor application of the sanctions; (iii) to measure their effects; (iv) to provide humanitarian assistance; and (v) to study possible ways of assisting Member States under Article 50 of the Charter. The sanctions committees set up by the Security Council in various instances to monitor application have in fact fulfilled certain of these tasks.

There are also long passages in the Agenda on coercive measures involving the use of force. Collective security, the principal innovation of the United Nations Charter, authorizes the Security Council to use force when peaceful measures have failed. We know, however, that Article 42, which provides the grounds for this action, has not been used by the Security Council due to the fact that the negotiations foreseen in Article 43 with a view to making armed forces available to the United Nations on a permanent basis were not able to be carried to their conclusion. This was due to opposition between the United States and the USSR at the beginning of the Cold War.

When the problem in the Persian Gulf between Kuwait and Iraq came to the point where force was needed, the Security Council preferred to authorize the Member States to take the necessary measures. There were serious questions about the legality of this act, and the least unsatisfactory justification which attempted to legitimize it was to place it within the context of legitimate collective self-defence under Article 51.

In 1992, the Secretary-General considered that the time had nevertheless come to take a new look at the provisions of the Charter, and that the obstacles that had arisen in the first years of the United Nations to implementing Article 43 no longer existed. As a consequence, the Agenda proposed that the Security Council should start negotiations, with the assistance of the Military Staff Committee; the Committee would thus be revived, and would no longer operate in the framework of peace-keeping operations but in that of Chapter VII of the Charter. The Secretary-General considered, therefore, that the fact that the Security Council would now be able to rely on immediately available forces was certain to have a dissuasive effect on a potential aggressor, at least in meeting any threat posed by a military force of a lesser order. However, the Security Council has clearly never taken to this approach; there has been no follow-up, and finally the system in Article 43 has never been negotiated, despite political conditions that might effectively appear more favourable.

Multiplying conflicts and the reticence of states to make forces available led to the pursuing of an idea launched in the Agenda, consisting in creating peace-enforcement units. These units – and the word 'enforcement' is clear in this respect – were not to be confused with the peace-keeping forces, and would respond to a specific need: cease-fire agreements are often made, only to be violated, and the United Nations is then called upon to restore and maintain them. Such a task can exceed the mission of the peace-keeping forces, or involve actions and risks exceeding those agreed to by contributing states. The solution would therefore lie in the availability of peace-enforcement units composed of voluntary troops supplied by Member States. The mandate of

An Agenda for Peace 31
as a new means
of settling conflicts

these units, which would be held in reserve, would be clearly defined. This proposal aimed, therefore, to create an entirely new force. They were not the armed forces of Article 43, which were to intervene in the case of aggression, neither were they the peace-keeping forces, which were less heavily armed. Finally, these units were not to be confused with the stand-by forces which governments can agree to keep in reserve, so as to contribute to possible peace-keeping operations. One example of the latter were the 1,200 men, who could be mobilized in forty-eight hours, that President Mitterrand of France offered to make available to the Secretary-General for keeping the peace. This suggestion did not, however, meet with the approval of the Security Council and the matter stopped there.

Chapter VII was disregarded during the Cold War and then rehabilitated with its ending. As with energy that has been bottled up for a long time and then suddenly freed, Chapter VII has been subject to real over-exploitation, raising certain questions that must be asked as soon as force is used. These questions, which are echoed in the Supplement to the Agenda, relate specifically to the fact that in Bosnia and Herzegovina the Security Council decided to authorize Member States, acting in their national capacity or through regional arrangements (NATO), to use force to ensure compliance with the ban on military flights and to discourage attacks against safe areas. It is true that the United Nations came out of the experience stronger, inasmuch as it had been able to use its enforcement capacity. On the other hand, the Organization's credibility is at great risk, as it can be perceived by certain parties as lacking in impartiality and as certain states may possibly misuse the system by using force for actions that were not envisaged at the outset by the Security Council.

Chapter VIb of the Charter and peace-keeping operations

Peace-keeping operations, which were not foreseen in the Charter and were created in empirical fashion to face circumstances, experienced a boom just after the end of the Cold War. In the Agenda mention is made of thirteen between 1945 and 1987 (i.e. in forty-two years), and thirteen others between 1987 and 1992 (i.e. in only five years). Their increase in numbers is not their only characteristic. Their increase in numbers of men, types of activity and therefore in cost, must also be underlined, the largest operation having been the peace-keeping operation in the former Yugoslavia. This situation has resulted in a certain number of constraints and difficulties which were predicted in the Agenda and which subsequent practice has confirmed, to the extent that nowadays this type of operation seems to have come to a standstill, with preference being given to other United Nations activities organized around a wider concept of peace, as we shall see later.

There have been several changes to peace-keeping operations, due to the fact that nowadays they concern domestic conflicts. The protagonists are often guerrillas, militia or armed civilians, with little or no discipline, making the United Nations' task very difficult. Conflicts of this type result in a need for humanitarian action, and here (and this is new) the United Nations is called upon to protect convoys and humanitarian operations. Finally, the Bosnia and Herzegovina conflict introduced something which had never been seen before: a peace-keeping operation . . . without peace, since UNPROFOR was deployed before the cease-fires were concluded, and that it had the impossible task of promoting these and therefore of remaining neutral and impartial without stopping the (unidentified) aggressor in order not to compromise its negotiating capacity. Nevertheless, as in Somalia, the additional mandates assigned for the operation demanded the use of force and had therefore moved away from the principles of consent, impartiality and the use of force limited to cases of legitimate defence. Nothing, however, is more dangerous than to expect a peace-keeping operation to use force, when it is neither technically nor in its concept equipped to do so. The logic behind peace-keeping is not that of coercive measures, and there is no continuum between the two.

Another alternative – a novelty at the time – was applied in Namibia, Angola, El Salvador, Cambodia and Mozambique – whereby the United Nations forces received a mandate to assist the parties in implementing the settlements that had been negotiated. In this way, the United Nations began to diversify its actions in the service of peace, a diversification that we shall return to later on.

Outlining the 'new departures in peace-keeping' the Secretary-General recalls the basic conditions for the success of these operations: 'a clear and practicable mandate; the co-operation of the parties in implementing that mandate; the continuing support of the Security Council; the readiness of Member States to contribute the military, police and civilian personnel,

An Agenda for Peace
as a new means
of settling conflicts   33

including specialists, required; effective United Nations command at Headquarters and in the field; and adequate financial and logistic support' (Agenda, paragraph 50). Peace-keeping operations have branched out and become more complex, and are no longer reduced – as was the case for the first among them – to providing a police force along a given border. These new peace-keeping operations, sometimes qualified as second- or even third-generation, have a considerably wider field of action which calls for many different kinds of personnel. Military staff will therefore be joined by civilians, including political specialists, human-rights observers, personnel in charge of elections, specialists in humanitarian aid and refugees, police, etc. Their number, training and equipment are complex, costly issues which must find practical solutions. The Agenda already underlined these constraints, which the operations in the former Yugoslavia later confirmed: simply to read the above-quoted conditions from paragraph 50 of the Agenda is to predict the outcome, since most of these conditions have not been met. In other operations, the impossibility with which the Secretary-General has been confronted of gathering the necessary troops within the required delay has led to a preferred technique of delegating to multinational or national forces as, for example, in Rwanda with operation Turquoise carried out by France, which was called upon as a national force when 'in May 1994 . . . not one of the 19 Governments that at that time had undertaken to have troops on stand-by agreed to contribute' (*Supplement to an Agenda for Peace*, paragraph 43). These operations also present the great advantage for the United Nations of relieving its budget, and practice over recent years has precisely consisted in using a technique that could be called 'sandwiching', in that it inserts a national or multinational operation between two United Nations peace-keeping operations. Thus, in Somalia there was 'Restore Hope' between UNOSOM I and UNOSOM II; in Rwanda, 'Turquoise' between UNAMIR I and UNAMIR II; and then in Haiti, 'Restore Democracy' between the two phases of UNMIH.

Finally, the importance of the passage in the Agenda where the Secretary-General insists on the need for a permanent stock of equipment to fill the gaps in certain under-equipped national units was confirmed some time later when UNPROFOR received under-equipped Pakistani troops. This delayed their participation in the theatre of operations by several months. Unfortunately, the General Assembly has never agreed to release the necessary funds to purchase such a permanent stock, with the result that the difficulties in this area are as bad as ever.

Chapter VIII of the Charter

For forty years, the omnipresence of the East–West relationship in many regional conflicts and the existence of certain specific political situations (such as Israel and South Africa) did not allow the procedures of Chapter VIII to be fully operational. Times have changed, and we realize that there are a great many conflicts that are in effect authentically regional. Recourse to Chapter VIII has therefore come to be seen as a necessity, all the more so since there is an additional, more technical and contingent, consideration. As the increase in number and the geographical dissemination of conflicts during the 1990s have prevented the United Nations from taking responsibility for all of them, it has become necessary to plan a better distribution of tasks.

Regional action, which has been called for on several occasions by the Secretary-General, is presented as a technique that can 'contribute to a deeper sense of participation, consensus and democratization in international affairs' (Agenda, paragraph 64). Apart from the traditional arguments focusing on the advantages of having the settlement body near by, and respect for local specificities, regional action is the only reasonable solution, bearing in mind the limited financial and material resources of the United Nations.

Task-sharing has therefore been attempted by the United Nations, with varying degrees of success. In Yugoslavia, the Secretary-General approached the European Union countries about the contributions they would be willing to make in the form of personnel, equipment and logistic support. Collaboration was established with the European Union through the Peace Conference, co-chaired by representatives of both organizations. The difficulties of this collaboration became evident during the summer of 1992 at a time when tension arose between the Security Council and the Secretary-General over the conflict in Bosnia and Herzegovina. At the time, the Secretary-General stressed that this conflict could draw the United Nations into actions exceeding their operational capacity and

An Agenda for Peace
as a new means
of settling conflicts   35

undertaken at the expense of their capacity to resolve other conflicts which were just as cruel and dangerous: Somalia, for example. Later, collaboration with NATO in the same conflict required detailed mechanisms for co-operation to be perfected (leading to the so-called 'double key' for air strikes), in view of the profound differences between the philosophies and cultures of the two organizations. In Somalia, collaboration was set up with the Arab League, the Organization of the Islamic Conference and the OAU. In Nagorny Karabakh, collaboration was with the OSCE. In the case of South Africa, after apartheid had been dismantled, the OAU, the British Commonwealth and the European Union were called upon to send observers within the framework of the National Peace Accord. This is also the interpretation that should be given to the position of the OSCE at the Helsinki Summit on 9 July 1992, when it announced its desire to co-operate with the United Nations in peace-serving actions, which it did in Yugoslavia, for example. In the case of Haiti, quite a complex system of collaboration was set up between the United Nations and the OAS.

It is not because it uses these different means, ranging from delegation to sub-contracting via decentralization, that the United Nations ceases to carry out its mission. The idea is not to relieve the Organization of its task, but to help it to fulfil it more successfully. In paragraph 86 of the *Supplement to an Agenda for Peace,* the Secretary-General defines five forms of possible co-operation between the United Nations and regional organizations: (i) consultation; (ii) diplomatic support (as with the OSCE in Nagorny Karabakh); (iii) operational support (as with NATO support for UNPROFOR in the former Yugoslavia); (iv) co-deployment (as with ECOWAS in Liberia or with the CIS in Georgia); (v) joint operations (as with the OAS in Haiti). In all cases, however, the primacy of the United Nations, as set out in the Charter, must be respected.

At the same time, in addition to recourse to regional bodies, which corresponds to territorial decentralization, the United Nations must also take steps for functional decentralization. This should enable the United Nations to count on various organizations for support. In this, the NGOs play an essential role, especially in the humanitarian area, where co-operation has been established (for example in channelling assistance, as was the case during the operations in Somalia or in Bosnia and Herzegovina). In order that the NGOs may play this important role to the full, proper co-ordination with the United Nations is necessary (*Supplement to an Agenda for Peace,* paragraph 89).

REINFORCING PEACE

However essential it may be, action to restore peace cannot guarantee, in today's closely interdependent world, that international safety will be established to last. Moreover, the polymorphous nature of peace, which is no longer limited as in the old days to the lack of war, is totally transforming the realities of United Nations action. In the modern world, weapons are no longer the only danger to peace. There are also under-development, damage to the environment and violations of democratic principles and human rights. This means that individuals are less frequently the victims of an enemy bullet than of torture, genocide and other forms of violent aggression, often perpetrated in their own countries and under the authority of their own governments.

Confronted with these situations, the United Nations cannot remain inactive. In the three Agendas, the Secretary-General considers most pertinently that in the current world, to live in peace means to be spared these new scourges. However, the latter are to a large degree interdependent. It is often following an armed conflict that serious economic difficulties arise and that state institutions are destroyed. But it is also because the structure of the state is weak or non-existent that a climate of violence and of conflict sets in, generating a breach of domestic security which can well spread to the whole of the region. Finally, who could deny that the gaps between the developed and developing world are a deep-seated factor of insecurity, or that for peace to exist there must be development?

In other words, it is no longer sufficient simply to stop conflicts once they have broken out. Their causes must be investigated much more thoroughly than in the past, and action taken while there is still time to remove them. And because, in the area of peace as in others, prevention is better than cure, peace-building aims essentially at organizing prevention. The idea, therefore, is to detect conflicts before they arise, using the techniques of preventive diplomacy. Furthermore, it is just as important to prevent a conflict, once settled, from arising again. To guard against this possibility, the United Nations is committed to the concept of post-conflict peace-building.

An Agenda for Peace 37
as a new means
of settling conflicts

Preventive diplomacy

The Secretary-General considers that 'the most desirable and efficient employment of diplomacy is to ease tensions before they result in conflict' (Agenda, paragraph 23). Preventive diplomacy can be undertaken by the Secretary-General himself, but also by the Security Council, the General Assembly and by regional organizations in co-operation with the United Nations. In a certain manner, diplomacy can be considered to be first and foremost, and by nature, preventive: effective diplomacy is in reality that which succeeds in detecting crises and tensions sufficiently in advance, and in defusing them before they degenerate into open conflict. The United Nations and its organs are, therefore, totally within their role, and the Secretary-General is certainly right to underline the importance of this element. However, the exercise of such preventive diplomacy calls for new measures, starting with the reorganization of the Secretariat by creating a Department of Political Affairs which is responsible for a range of political functions that were formerly dispersed among several departments. This department now has the means to follow political developments worldwide, so that it can detect emerging zones of tension in time to plan preventive measures. More generally, the exercise of preventive diplomacy requires easy access to information as well as fact-finding procedures so that the accuracy of this information can be checked. The establishment of an early warning system is also a basic element for success.

The importance of information

In a world with so many ultra-sophisticated and efficient information techniques, the United Nations is particularly ill-equipped. It is in fact dependent upon the Member States which, thanks, for example, to their observation satellites, possess information that they can choose to communicate, or not to communicate, to the Secretary-General of the United Nations. (The Organization itself has no observation satellites, and Javier Pérez de Cuéllar deplored their absence when Kuwait was invaded by Iraq.) One cannot help being struck by the almost antiquated means with which the United Nations has to operate, while at the same it is called upon to do so much!

Basically, the success of preventive diplomacy lies in mutual trust. Trust first of all between Member States who wish to act jointly in order that the peace may not be breached. Then trust between the Member States and the United Nations so that states provide the Organization with the means to achieve its aims. The process of confidence- and security-building, to use an expression from the final act of Helsinki, is widely used today as a diplomatic tool for disarmament, peace-keeping and co-operation. The Secretary-General also refers to these measures in the Agenda and considers that an element of good faith is essential to reduce the risks of conflicts between states.

However, for such measures to be usefully implemented, the true facts need to be known. Everyone is aware of the importance of this element in solving conflicts. There are indeed many situations that arise, persist and deteriorate because there has been an error, or ignorance at the outset of the actual facts. The General Assembly did in fact underline this by adopting Declaration 46/59 of 19/12/1991 on 'Fact-finding by the United Nations in the Field of the Maintenance of International Security'. With the importance of this principle thus accepted, its methods of application are varied. They enable the best possible use to be made of the competences of the Secretary-General (better equipped now to use Article 99 of the Charter) and of United Nations bodies such as the General Assembly and the Security Council in actions to keep the peace.

Various types of inquiries can be carried out, including the fact-finding missions which the General Assembly and the Security Council can send under their authority. In some instances even, the presence of such a mission can help to defuse a dispute. Naturally, when the representatives of the United Nations are sent to gather information in a given territory, there are necessary meetings and conversations with political leaders, during which solutions may be found which remove the threats to international security. The impact of these effects will be greatest when the Security Council decides, as it can in exceptional circumstances, to meet away from Headquarters. When this occurs, not only can it take a closer look at the situation, but also demonstrate its authority. In this way, fact-finding procedures can even help to settle a dispute which they were originally only intended to clarify.

Nevertheless, the success of preventive diplomacy does not lie merely in providing complete and reliable information. This is just an essential preliminary step in exercising a role which rests above all on the goodwill of Member States

An Agenda for Peace
as a new means
of settling conflicts   39

and their sincere will to come to a peaceful solution that demonstrates their desire for peace. Unfortunately, states are not always willing to accept the assistance of the United Nations, particularly in domestic matters. These come less obviously within the competence of the Organization, and action must therefore comply with the provisions of Article 2, paragraph 7 of the Charter. On this point, the Secretary-General wonders whether the best solution in the long term might not be in 'creating a climate of opinion, or ethos, within the international community in which the norm would be for Member States to accept an offer of United Nations good offices' (*Supplement to an Agenda for Peace,* paragraph 28), which is another way of expressing the idea of developing a 'culture of peace'.

These various procedures, which can also be used when tensions have already appeared, have been complemented with other mechanisms which are more typically characteristic of preventive diplomacy. Of note are the early warning systems, which are a particularly innovative proposal in the Agenda. These systems have to form a real United Nations 'network' able to sound the alarm by broadcasting immediate information in the event of various kinds of danger: environmental threats, natural disasters, the risk of nuclear accident or other risks affecting the life or health of populations. These systems, which require close co-operation between the departments of the Secretariat and the Specialized Agencies, enable information to be used in the best possible manner. They also require the participation of regional organizations, in particular those with observer status which are therefore linked with the security mechanisms of the United Nations.

Yet preventive diplomacy goes beyond mere information, and can be accompanied by actions in the field aiming to curb conflicts.

Curbing conflicts

In such cases, preventive diplomacy takes the form of what the Agenda calls preventive deployment, which can be organized by the United Nations once conflict has broken out. In this aspect, therefore, such missions are totally traditional and, where conflicts between states are concerned, follow the same logic as that followed by the peace-keeping operations when they set up a buffer force to prevent direct confrontations between the parties concerned, such as in

Suez in 1956, when the United Nations Emergency Force was deployed on Egyptian territory with the agreement of the government. On the basis of this tried and tested formula, all sorts of combinations are clearly possible, whether the conflict has already broken out or is simply feared. In the latter case, nothing prevents the state from asking the United Nations to provide protection by setting up preventive deployment on its territory (at its border, for example) so as to deter feared hostilities. An example of this was the action taken in the former Yugoslav Republic of Macedonia, where the dissuasive effect of deploying part of UNPROFOR, then of UNPREDEP, proved its worth, with the result that the country was spared the conflict which had such serious consequences for the neighbouring republics of the former Yugoslavia. On several occasions, moreover, the Secretary-General underlined this application of the preventive deployment concept in his reports concerning the conflicts of the former Yugoslavia.

The principal originality of the Agenda in this area lies in the fact that it also takes into account new, domestic conflicts, which have been increasing at a worrying rate over the last few years. The main difficulty, therefore, is the requirement concerning the consent of the relevant state to such operations, so that its sovereignty is preserved. It is humanitarian assistance that is mostly involved here, organized in strict compliance with the principles defined by resolution 46/182 of 19/12/1991 (improved co-ordination of United Nations emergency humanitarian assistance), which concern the agreement of the parties and respect for the humanitarian, neutral and impartial nature of such assistance.

Finally, another form of concrete action for preventive diplomacy consists in demilitarizing a zone with a view to separating potential belligerents and keeping the peace and security in a sensitive region. For example, in 1992, during the conflicts in the former Yugoslavia, demilitarization of the Prevlaka peninsula was carried out with the agreement of the parties.

Post-conflict peace-building

This is surely the most interesting novelty in *An Agenda for Peace,* and is proof of the United Nations' will to support and accompany peace. Once peace has been restored, it must be made to last. In this sense, peace-building is also connected with preventive diplomacy. The latter aims to prevent the occurrence of a conflict

An Agenda for Peace 41
as a new means
of settling conflicts

that has not yet arisen. Peace-building aims at preventing the re-emergence of an earlier conflict that has been settled by a procedure and has resulted in peace. Both are preventive actions aiming to consolidate peace and make it lasting.

In the aftermath of domestic conflicts that, as we have said, are on the increase, this lasting peace requires stable institutions, established after free and honest elections organized in compliance with human rights and with the rule of law. In the aftermath of an international conflict, peace-making presupposes a network of economic co-operation with other states so that institutions affected by the conflict can be restored, confidence regained and development enhanced.

Political development as a peace-building process

All these actions, some of which aim at furthering political development and democracy, and others at ensuring economic development and social well-being, will come within the United Nations' responsibility under the heading of peace-building. United Nations' action obviously requires the consent of the state for the actual implementation of the reconstruction process. However, on the basis of Chapter VII and thus avoiding the obstacle of Article 2, paragraph 7, it is also possible for the United Nations to decide upon actions that constitute a platform on which a constitutional state can then be built. Thus, in the case of Haiti, resolution 940 of 31/7/1994, on the basis of Chapter VII of the Charter, proposed a rehabilitation of the political situation, authorizing the use of 'all necessary means' to make the junta leave so that the elected President might return. It is evident that, without this precondition, nothing could have been democratically built upon the platform prepared by the action undertaken on the basis of Chapter VII.

In addition, when the restoration of the state is part of a process whereby peace returns under the responsibility of the United Nations, the latter can act on its own initiative. For example, in Somalia, the Secretary-General stated that while humanitarian operations in the country as a whole would continue, activities to rebuild the state of Somalia could begin in regions where stability and security had definitely been established.

Finally, the fact that action for restoring the state is one component in a peace-keeping and peace-building operation both simplifies and complicates matters. It simplifies matters because the restoration will operate along traditional lines that have been proved by collaboration with states providing the necessary staff (which, moreover, no longer consists only of military personnel, but also includes civilians who ensure respect for human rights, provide humanitarian assistance or participate in rebuilding constitutional or administrative aspects of the state). As for the complications, they lie in the fact that this specific action is not always easy to identify within an operation as a whole, either in its development or in the methods used.

Indeed, one can wonder when, in certain cases, an operation to restore the state starts and when it ends. It is not always easy to answer the question of when it starts. Mention was made above of a platform, upon which the constitutional state can then be built; but in order to rebuild on firm foundations, it is first necessary to raze the old building to the ground. This precondition, however, may go back a long way, for example to an embargo aimed at bringing the government of the time to repent, or even to leave. Is what we have here simply a peace-keeping operation or is it already part of an operation to restore the state? As for the end of an operation, it is of course possible to say that it comes when the last United Nations staff member has left the territory, and when the institutions of the restored state take the destiny of the country into their hands. This is the case, for example, of Cambodia. If we look no further, the United Nations action in Cambodia was a success. If we look at the aftermath, after the United Nations left, we have to be more circumspect and maybe even qualify our opinion of the Organization's action to rebuild the state. Should not the success of the operation also be judged over a certain period following restoration, just as an architect or builder is still responsible for what he has built for some time after its completion? And indeed, although it is not possible to talk of responsibility in the legal sense, the United Nations has admitted that it cannot remain indifferent to the follow-up of its action. This consideration was specifically put forward in the case of Haiti, stating that the United Nations, which had enabled the election of Jean-Bertrand Aristide, could not stand by and witness his overthrow without reacting. It feels bound, therefore, to provide an after-sales service (if such a frivolous term can be allowed).

The lengthy duration of an operation to rebuild the state has, in several cases, led the United Nations to transfer responsibility to the UNDP, the appropriate

An Agenda for Peace   43
as a new means
of settling conflicts

agency to take on this kind of massive programme. Thus, for Haiti, important UNDP initiatives concerned the exercise of authority, human development, reform of the state and humanitarian assistance. Economic, social and environmental projects can be added to the above institutional initiatives. In Rwanda, the UNDP devised projects to help in formulating and funding a general plan to rehabilitate the country and restore the administrative infrastructure, in particular regarding assistance to refugees and displaced persons within the country.

In this way, we can observe the complex relay system between states and the Organization, and within the United Nations system itself, from one agency to another. If, as we have seen, the weight of the operation and its duration justify it being passed on at a given moment to the UNDP, we can consider that the operation then leaves the area of peace once this has been restored, to enter the more mundane field of technical assistance.

Actions and their contents

What are these actions to restore the state? The aim is to re-establish the rules and institutions which have been damaged or destroyed – as if the state were a building to be restored – by organizing all kinds of political, economic and social activities which can help to establish or re-establish a democratically chosen government and provide it with the means of action for managing the state. The best way to start is without doubt by monitoring electoral procedures, as fair elections will allow leaders to be chosen democratically, and this is a prerequisite for all subsequent action to restore the state. Then comes constitutional and administrative assistance, which will provide the state with the judicial resources it needs in order to act legally. Once these legal frameworks have been reinstated, the country's recovery is made possible by arrangements for the return of refugees and their social reintegration, assistance to the population and mine-clearing operations: in short, by a range of social measures that are necessary, albeit not sufficient, for economic development. Neither must we forget the essential financial support of the Bretton Woods institutions, without which our arguments on recovery would have little chance of proving themselves in practice.

In theory, despite the fact that the law appears here as an infrastructure, the above model is coherent. Observation of practice results in a more qualified opinion of its value. The opinion must be qualified primarily in the light of existing or expected results: none of the cases in which it has been applied have been a success. Serious reservations are justified, whether for Cambodia, Somalia, Angola, Mozambique or Haiti. Judgement must also be qualified by questioning, which is indispensable, albeit all too rare, of the relevance of the proposed models when the restoration of the state is put into practice. Questions on the universality or relativity of its operating rules cannot be avoided. For as long as it existed, Marxist criticism of liberal doctrine had the advantage of forming a counter-balance which led to the necessary investigation of other possible choices. Because Marxism has been wrongly identified with Soviet ideology, the disappearance of the USSR has resulted in 'the baby being thrown away with the bath water'. As a result the transposition of the liberal model goes unquestioned. We know, however, that the model of a constitutional state is not necessarily universally suitable, and that this model runs the serious risk of remaining mere words if it is just an empty shell. The question, therefore, is less that of institutions as they are described on paper than that of their adaptation to a social reality that differs from the one for which they were conceived. The possibilities of emancipation from foreign systems are limited, particularly when such emancipation would be at the cost of risking international isolation. In order to avoid this, states have had to keep up appearances. The main risk here, then, is that the international community (and not only the United Nations) can only help in providing window dressing, without being able to take care of what is inside the shop. In this case, there will only be the outer appearance of a constitutional state, with very little content.

But are the systems proposed still adapted to the context in which they are used? And is universality appropriate in this field? Article 21, paragraph 3 of the Universal Declaration of Human Rights lays down the principle of universal suffrage. Is it an insult to the idea of democracy to consider that the meaning of suffrage can vary according to economic, social and cultural factors, and also to the values and beliefs to which a given society is attached, and that such a society might better express these through other techniques? The Secretary-General is quite clear on this point: the United Nations cannot and must not impose anything in this respect. 'Rather, the United Nations aims to help each state

An Agenda for Peace   45
as a new means
of settling conflicts

pursue its own particular path' (*An Agenda for Democratization,* paragraph 11). Indeed, in paragraph 10, he stresses that

each society must be able to choose the form, pace and character of its democratization process. Imposition of foreign models not only contravenes the Charter principle of non-intervention in internal affairs, it may also generate resentment among both the Government and the public, which may in turn feed internal forces inimical to democratization and to the idea of democracy.

This action is not without risks, and the same *Agenda for Democratization* pinpoints these in paragraph 20 as follows:

It is true that the introduction of democratic practices into formerly authoritarian or war-torn states may contribute to civil conflict by opening channels for free expression, including the expression of hatred. Free and fair elections can be followed by the suppression of those defeated. There is also a danger that strengthening civil society without also addressing state capacity may undermine governability or overwhelm the state. Especially for Governments in underdeveloped countries, which are typically engaged full time in the provision of basic human needs for their populations, the risks to stability that may arise in the early stages of democratization may make them reluctant to continue democratization or even to begin the process at all.

Whatever the outcome of these questionings, in practice, the development of operations to restore the state is remarkable. Demands for assistance with elections show a sharp increase. The same applies to constitutional and administrative assistance for building a constitutional state. United Nations action in these fields – while it is not exclusive, since other agencies also participate – presents certain specific advantages in comparison with other actions. Election-monitoring stamped with the United Nations label produces certified, non-contested results in compliance with democratic principles. As for the constitutional and administrative assistance provided by the United Nations, it is also more likely to be perceived as more neutral and objective, and less marked by the transfer of a given model or by ulterior political motives. And it is true that the adoption of a given administrative model in preference to another can have consequences later in affecting the choices and behaviour of decision-makers.

It can be assumed that if the Organization is increasingly active in the area of settling conflicts it is because this action responds to a new and very definitely expressed need on the part of the Member States. The fact that this need is new does not affect the permanence of the concepts of United Nations peace missions, but the fact that the need is new calls for a change of methods, whence their expansion to include areas for which the connection with peace and the settlement of conflicts was not established at the outset as clearly as it is in the Agendas and, more particularly, in the first of the three: *An Agenda for Peace.*

Pacific settlement of conflict: the role of the United Nations

Takashi Inoguchi

INTRODUCTION

Some forty years ago Kenneth Waltz defined the causes for the recurrence of war as originating in people's minds, in the nature of the state, and in the balance of power among nations.[1] He draws on the writings of philosophers to examine systematically how these three causal images relate to the occurrence of war. The first image is of the human mind as the principal cause of war. Hence the famous phrase in UNESCO's Constitution, 'wars begin in the minds of men'. The second image is of the state that resorts to war out of the instinct for self-aggrandizement: the state as a war machine with bad intentions. The third image is of the configuration of international power itself as a major cause of the outbreak of war. International relations, the argument goes, are inherently unstable and inclined to lead to war.

Peter Gourevitch reverses the causal arrow with respect to the second image, arguing that war often shakes and shapes the characteristics of the state.[2] War often changes the nature of a political system. Arthur Stein and Bruce Russett point out that in all the seven major wars of the nineteenth and twentieth centuries, vanquished nations had to change the features of their political systems

---

1. Kenneth Waltz, *Man, the State and War,* New York, Columbia University Press, 1958.
2. Peter Gourevitch, 'The Second Image Reversed: The International Sources of Domestic Politics', *International Organization,* Vol. 32, No. 4, Autumn 1978, pp. 881–912.

to harmonize with those of the victorious nations.[3] War often changes economic systems, too. The defeat of the South in the American Civil War of the mid-nineteenth century halted the flow of agricultural products from the southern states to Europe, a breach quickly filled by South American agriculture. From then onward the South was steadily marginalized within the economy of the United States and the world.

One wonders why the first and third images of the occurrence of war have not been proposed in reverse à la Peter Gourevitch. The first image reversed would mean the outbreak of war causing changes in people's mental framework in a negative direction. Cases in point would be the conflicts in Bosnia and Herzegovina, and Rwanda which have produced tremendous mental distress in the children who were victims of those conflicts. The third image reversed would evoke the reconfigurations and changes in the framework of international relations caused by war. This would explain why peace tends to prevail after major conflicts like the Napoleonic Wars and the Second World War.

These three images of war and their reverse images may enable us to see a larger horizon of the pacific settlement of conflicts. What I propose to do here is to examine systematically what methods of pacific conflict settlement can be envisaged in each of the six causal images introduced above.

PACIFIC SETTLEMENT OF CONFLICT

The first image prescribes the transformation of people's mental framework. The second image prescribes the transformation of the nature of a regime. The third image prescribes a transformation in the nature of international relations and the world economy. Let us first take a closer look at each of the three and then examine the causal arguments applying to the reversed images.

Once people's mental framework is predisposed to war, whether out of general distrust, desire for revenge, or as a manifestation of aggression or greed, war is more likely to take place according to this image. To remedy this, we need

---

3.   Arthur Stein and Bruce Russett, 'Consequences of War'. In: Robert Ted Gurr (ed.), *Handbook of Political Conflict*, New York, Free Press, 1980.

Pacific settlement
of conflict: the role
of the United Nations

49

to study the psychological mechanisms through which people reach a decision to enter into war. Understanding this image therefore draws on the science of psychology and other behavioural sciences. Peace education is necessary to inculcate the norms and culture of peace.

The pacific settlement of conflict in this image thus relies on efforts to change people's perspectives, mental framework and predispositions so as to make war seem like a less palatable instrument for conflict resolution. A couple of instances will illustrate this.

First, let us consider the Bosnian peace negotiations held in Dayton, Ohio, in 1996. The three negotiators from Bosnia and Herzegovina faced a formidable American negotiator named Richard Holbrooke. The Bosnian representatives were exposed to relentless pressure to sign the peace agreement drafted by the United States. They wanted to go home even without a peace agreement. But Richard Holbrooke would not give them a return ticket and is said to have in fact locked them in the hotel where the negotiations took place. Rumour has it that he told them that if they wanted to go home, they would have to sign the agreement first, like it or not. Ultimately they did. If this is indeed what happened, it represents the practice of the first image by associating the continuation of war with the painful experience of being relentlessly bullied, and a peace agreement with release from the bully.

A second instance is the peace conference held in Tokyo prior to the Cambodian Peace Agreement of 1993. At the first assembly of the three parties involved in the war, Japan pledged that once peace was agreed upon, it would offer each party an amount in development assistance larger than they had ever heard of in their lives. In this instance, peace was associated with economic assistance, and the continuation of war with its refusal. Although initially deeply suspicious of each other and rightly sceptical of the prospect of actually receiving such economic assistance, the three war parties came to see this 'carrot' as possibly leading to their respective gains in the future. This illustrates the first image by associating continuing the war with no money and a peace agreement with money poured into Cambodia.

The second image prescribes a change of regimes. Thus after the Russian February Revolution of 1917, Leon Trotsky proclaimed 'neither war nor peace', calling for more revolutionary changes of regime on both sides of the war front, in Russia and Germany.[4] Continuation of war would mean acceptance of the Menshevik and imperial regimes in Russia and Germany. Peace would mean the defeat of Russia and the acceptance of the Menshevik regime. What Trotsky wanted was a revolution across borders to oust the 'decadent' regimes on both sides of the war. He called for an international Communist revolution that would bring about a more solid and lasting change of regimes to correspond to his vision.

The debate on democratic peace originating with Immanuel Kant's 1795 tract, *For Perpetual Peace*, also makes use of the second image.[5] 'Democracies rarely fight each other', he observes concisely. Democratic regimes require transparency and accountability to the public. This requirement makes it much more difficult for them to resort to war. When those conditions are doubled – since war involves at least two parties – democracies can be seen historically to fight each other very rarely. Furthermore, the awareness among democracies that they share a common set of values and norms makes it even less likely that they would declare war among themselves. This is not very different from Trotsky's vision that solidarity due to shared values and norms would ostensibly foster peace among Communist regimes.

The tenets of American foreign policy under the Clinton administration, as articulated in the President's State of the Union Address in 1994, stipulate democratization as one of its important pillars of diplomacy. The logic behind this stance is that further democratization creates a world where fighting is reduced at least among democracies and that, when democratic regimes prevail worldwide, war itself will be less likely to take place. Strobe Talbott, Deputy Secretary of State, describes it succinctly:

---

4 .   Leon Trotsky, *Permanentnacia Revolutsiia* [The Permanent Revolution], Moscow, Iskre Research, 1994.

5.   Immanuel Kant, *Perpetual Peace: A Philosophical Essay* (1903 edition), Thoemnes Antiqueria Books, 1996. See also Bruce Russett, *Grasping the Democratic Peace*, Princeton, Princeton University Press, 1993.

Pacific settlement
of conflict: the role
of the United Nations

51

In an increasingly interdependent world Americans have a growing stake in how other countries govern, or misgovern, themselves. The larger and more close-knit the community of nations that choose democratic forms of government, the safer and more prosperous Americans will be, since democracies are demonstratively more likely to maintain their international commitments, less likely to engage in terrorism or wreak environmental danger, and less likely to make war on each other.[6]

In the early 1970s, only thirty-odd countries were democracies. In the late 1990s more than 100 countries are regarded as democracies. One can argue that if all 185 Member States of the United Nations were democracies, the chances of war would become indeed rare.

The third image is linked to changes in the framework of international relations and the world economy. In place of the international anarchy that is said to prevail in international relations, institutionalists have been arguing that building blocs based on international accords would pave the way for peace because the behaviour of states would be more constrained by the web of transnational agreements.[7] This is the argument advanced to contain the unlawful behaviour in which states without such conflict-resolution mechanisms might be more inclined to indulge. Such mechanisms include accords concerning the treatment of prisoners of war, nuclear non-proliferation and ozone-layer protection.

This is Grotian rather than Hobbesian international relations. It is also Kantian. This image is sometimes called idealist, in contrast to realist. Idealism assumes that international accords and institutions exercise a certain constraining power, whereas realism assumes anarchy and trusts nothing other than power and wise judgement based on vested interests.[8] Indeed, in his empirical analysis of the relationship between the proliferation and framing influence of international organizations, Bruce Russett argues that the power of international organizations is conducive to peace. This may be called a legalist peace.[9]

---

6.   Strobe Talbott, as quoted in *The Economist*, 23 November 1996, p. 23.
7.   Robert Keohane, *After Hegemony*, Cambridge, Mass., Harvard University Press, 1981.
8 .   Kenneth Waltz, *Theory of International Politics*, New York, McGraw-Hill, 1979.
9 .   Bruce Russett, in a forthcoming article on the subject.

Likewise, to prevent the tyranny of the market, the World Trade Organization (WTO) sponsors quite solid mechanisms of dispute settlement not only in world trade, but also in wide-ranging related areas such as financial services, energy, communications, transportation, direct investment and intellectual property rights. In comparison to its predecessor, the General Agreement on Tariffs and Trade (GATT), it acts promptly and decides quickly in order to allow settlement of disputes to take place expeditiously and free trade to flourish. The metamorphosis from GATT to WTO was prompted by the globalization and liberalization of economic activity, which requires a good framework for transnational and transregional dispute settlement.[10]

This is in the Smithian rather than the non-Smithian tradition, with its isolationist, protectionist or blocist proclivities. In nineteenth-century English parlance, peace dovetails with free trade. In twentieth-century jargon, the network of interdependence creates islands of peace, which may come to encompass the entire globe in tandem with globalization and liberalization. Again, Bruce Russett argues, on the basis of the causal examination of the relationship between economic interdependence and peace, that the higher economic interdependence is, the greater the likelihood that peace will permeate the countries concerned. This is what he calls a liberal peace.[11]

THE ROLE OF THE UNITED NATIONS

Let us now turn to the role of the United Nations in the pacific settlement of conflict, as envisaged in the context of the three images.

The role of international organizations in the first image is to enlighten the public and disseminate the findings of psychological and behavioural sciences as to how certain human mind-sets make war more likely and aggravate the damage caused by it. This is exactly the role of UNESCO as enshrined in its Constitution:

---

10. Douglas A. Irwin, *Against the Tide: An Intellectual History of Free Trade*, Princeton, Princeton University Press, 1996.
11. John R. Oneal, Frances H. Oneal and Bruce Russett, 'The Liberal Peace: Interdependence, Democracy, and International Conflict, 1950–85', *Journal of Peace Research*, Vol. 33, No. 1, February 1996.

Pacific settlement
of conflict: the role
of the United Nations   53

'Since wars begin in the minds of men, it is in the minds of men that the defences of peace must be constructed.'

In the civil war in El Salvador, which lasted from 1980 to 1992, both sides planted land mines almost everywhere. The United Nations Children's Fund (UNICEF) played an important role in both clearing the country of these deadly mines and in raising awareness of their danger.[12] Mines tend to be harmless-looking in shape and catch the interest of people, especially children, who are unaware of their danger. Children will go and play wherever their curiosity takes them. So death and casualty figures among children are noticeably higher than among adults. In the civil war period between 1980 and 1992 several hundred children were killed each year by land mines. After the peace agreement, de-mining operations began. UNICEF set up programmes to educate people, especially children, about the danger of mines. Children learned about mines even before learning to read and write. Nationwide campaigns led by both the government and the Farabundo Marti National Liberation Front (FMLN) through radio and newspapers were not enough. For a period of fourteen months after the peace agreement, 3,600 volunteers spoke to 44 per cent of the population in high-risk areas. UNICEF was also able to arrange for participation of a Belgian business firm in the government/FMLN's joint de-mining operations.

The role of international organizations in the second image is to facilitate democratization through awakening and enlightening the public about democracy and the key common values associated with it. A series of large-scale, United Nations-organized conferences such as the Beijing Conference on Women, the Copenhagen Summit on Social Development and the Rio Earth Summit were all intended as devices to enlighten the public at large and to prod Member States into taking appropriate measures and passing legislation to effectuate key common values. The Office of the High Commissioner for Human Rights (OHCHR) is a United Nations body to promote human rights in order to prevent violations of human rights and to get Member States to take appropriate action. The International Research and Training Institute for the Advancement of Women (INSTRAW) is a United Nations body devoted to the advancement of the status

---

12.   UNICEF, *The State of the World's Children*, New York, UNICEF, 1996.

and role of women. The *Human Development Report* of the United Nations Development Programme (UNDP) registers indicators for all Member States not only in terms of economic, financial and technological development but also in terms of equality of life and representation.

International organizations do occasionally take actions that were intended to convince Member States to mend their ways, such as economic sanctions and military intervention. The former is more frequent than the latter, and is normally conducted in conjunction with military initiatives by Member States such as the United States. With regard to the United Nations, there remains some doubt as to the effectiveness of economic[13] and military sanctions;[14] nevertheless, they are examples of what the Organization can do to change the nature of wrongful political and economic practices of Member States. It should be noted that the United Nations does much less in the area of direct action, as envisaged in the second image, than in consciousness-raising and educational initiatives.

The role of international organizations in the third image is to facilitate 'less anarchy' in international relations and 'less tyranny' in the world market. By less anarchy I mean a more constructive framework of conflict resolution and mitigation than is currently practised. By less tyranny I mean a more humane framework for absorbing and adjusting to global market forces than is possible under a perfectly functioning market framework.

Less anarchical international relations can be achieved in two ways: communitarian and institutional. The former emphasizes the nurturing of a sense of the community of humankind, while the latter stresses the building of forums and networks and the binding of members with international accords. An example of the former is the keynote message of the Rio Earth Summit in which the perceived oneness in the face of damaged environments was cited in the endeavour to unite everyone on earth to collective action. An example of the latter is the institutionalization of the Law of the Sea: a process born out of the United Nations system to create guidelines for utilization of maritime resources. It

---

13. Gary Clyde Hufbamer et al., *Economic Sanctions Reconsidered*, 2nd ed., Institute of International Economics, 1990; Lisa Martin, *Coercive Currents*, PUP, 1992.

14. James Mayall, *The New International 1991–1994: United Nations Experience in Cambodia, former Yugoslavia and Rwanda*, Cambridge, Cambridge University Press, 1996.

Pacific settlement
of conflict: the role
of the United Nations

55

lasted for two decades or so and ended up as an independent international institution, headquartered in Kingston, Jamaica. In practice, communitarian and institutional methods are sometimes difficult to distinguish because their organizing principles of action are often mobilized simultaneously.

The tyranny of the global market can be alleviated in two ways in the third image. Again they are communitarian and institutionalist. The key slogan of the non-aligned countries in the 1970s was the New International Economic Order whereby they demanded a series of actions on the part of the industrialized countries of the North to remedy and rectify a world economy unfairly favourable to the North. This is communitarian in the sense that the unity and solidarity of the Group of 77 against the North in gap-mitigating political action was presumed to keep the North at bay. The institutional method is illustrated by the process by which the Uruguay Round of GATT evolved into the creation of the World Trade Organization. Facing the increasing economic interdependence and further globalization and liberalization of economic activities throughout the world, designing the guidelines and rules for much freer trade and more user-friendly dispute-settlement mechanisms became the *sine qua non* of such an organization. GATT was given its death sentence and the WTO created, albeit not *de novo*.

THE THREE IMAGES REVERSED

For each of the three images, there is a different standard liberal internationalist answer to the question of how conflict can be made amenable to pacific settlement. For the first image, the answer is peace research and education; for the second, democratization and market liberalization; for the third, formation of a global community and institutionalization. In this section I would like to examine these propositions, focusing on the practical role played by the United Nations.

I begin by examining the three images reversed, because it is an exercise that reveals the interactive causal mechanisms of the occurrence of war. In other words, pointing out one causal mechanism may not be sufficient to increase and enhance the possibilities for the pacific settlement of conflict. The first image reversed means that outbreak of war further determines and fixates the mind-set of affected people in the direction of more suspicion and a mentality that is more prone to resort to war.[15] Here peace research and education would have a very difficult time overcoming the amoral pragmatism pervasive among antagonistic peoples. The prevailing attitude in this vicious kind of world gives peace education and research a hollow ring. This counter-argument may be summed up by the word 'cynicism'.

The second image reversed means that war determines the polity and the economy of the vanquished countries to such a significant extent that their frameworks become heavily dependent on those projected or imposed on them by the victorious country. If the systems of a hegemonic country, whether they be democracy and a market economy, prevail in many other parts of the world as a result of victories in war or through the bandwagonning of smaller countries in the wake of the outcome of hegemonic war, then that could be an easy way to promote the pacific settlement of conflicts. The problem is that the hegemonic framework may not be democratic with a market economy in the first place. If it runs counter to democratization and market liberalization, then the second image and its approach to pacific settlement of conflict will not be very useful. This is the globalists' argument. In a nutshell they believe that the global framework determines the local framework, be it political or economic.[16] The counter-argument here is the perspective of globalism.

The third image reversed is of war that reinforces a more anarchical situation. Whether anarchy results in greater peace following great turmoil is arguable. The sporadic tinkering by international institutions may not be the most expedient way of realizing peace if greater anarchy is more likely to bring about peace through the mechanisms of balance of power or through the bandwagonning of minor powers within the framework of a hegemonic power. The essence of this argument is that peace is achieved by war or at least by good war preparedness.[17] Counter-arguments along these lines may be categorized as realism.

---

15. UNICEF, op. cit., note 12.
16. Robert Gilpin, *War and Change in World Politics*, New York, Cambridge University Press, 1981.
17. Henry Kissinger, *Diplomacy*, New York, Simon & Schuster, 1994.

Pacific settlement   57
of conflict: the role
of the United Nations

POST-COLD WAR CONTENTION OF THE SIX SCHOOLS OF THOUGHT

The counter-arguments of cynicism, globalism and realism against the three images envisaged by Kenneth Waltz in the form of pacifism (the sentiment for peace brings about peace), nationalism (national determination prevails in the framework of the nation-state), and institutionalism (by building blocs of peace anarchistic icebergs can be melted), respectively cannot be underevaluated. The world has been awash with these three terms since the end of the Cold War.

The post-Cold War period has showcased all six of these mental frameworks, like the proverbial 'one hundred flowers blooming, one hundred schools contending'. If people of the peace-dividend persuasion are committed to peace, peace should prevail. The Economists Allied for Arms Reduction (ECAAR) advances the argument with a set of interesting models and references. In reality, much of what the peace dividenders wanted to see was not realized. James Baker, former US Secretary of State, noted during the transition period of 1989 to 1992 that substantial arms reduction should not be carried out since the aura of uncertainty counselled the United States to retain much of its military might in order to retain its primacy in world affairs.[18]

Like isolationists, people pay less attention to international affairs in the absence of one overarching enemy. That is why it is convenient for the globalists to find common menaces in Islamic fundamentalism, the China factor, international terrorism and nuclear proliferation.[19] Some even go so far as to call the post-Cold War a one-superpower world and the twenty-first century another American century, granting much smaller room for manoeuvre for the rest of the world. Confidence- and institution-building measures were first enthusiastically advanced in many parts of the world, especially in the immediate post-Cold War

18. James Baker, *The Politics of Diplomacy: Revolution, War and Peace, 1989–1994*, New York, G. P. Putnam's Sons, 1995.
19. Samuel Huntington, *The Clash of Civilizations and the Remaking of World Order*, New York, Simon & Schuster, 1996; James Shinn (ed.), *Weaving the Net*, New York, Council on Foreign Relations Press, 1995; Lea Brilmayer, *American Hegemony: Political Monopoly in a One-Superpower World*, New Haven, Yale University Press, 1994; Alfredo Valladao, *The 21st Century Will be an American Century*, London, Verso, 1996.

transition of 1989 to 1992. It was the time when two institutions emerged: the World Trade Organization created by the Uruguay Round and the European Union created by the Treaty of Maastricht. It was the time when the United States and the United Nations got along well with each other in Iraq, in Cambodia and elsewhere. But with time there has been a resurgence of the realists, who are once again asserting themselves in downplaying efforts along institutional policy lines. Hence the cloud over European Monetary Union; hence the cloud over the United Nations; hence the cloud over the Asia Pacific Economic Co-operation (APEC) forum; hence the cloud over the Korean Energy Development Organization (KEDO).

CONCLUSION

Building on the above analysis, my conclusions focus on the role of the United Nations. I would rank the Organization's performance in its three major roles as follows: best performance is in consciousness-raising and inculcation of norms; second best, formulation of frameworks, guidelines and rules, and provision of goods and services; and third, imposition of sanctions. This rank order does not seem to have changed with the end of the Cold War. Rather, despite all the difficulties encountered over the last few years – or even because of them – the United Nations will continue to play a role that cannot be dismissed outright, especially in the first and second categories.

New international approaches to the solution of ethnic problems in Central Europe

Rudolf Joo and Reka Szemerkenyi

FROM PEACE BY CONTAINMENT TO PEACE BY CONVICTION

Few political phenomena in the world have received such extremely opposing assessments in the past few years as the national/ethnic reawakening of the 1990s in Central Europe.[1] The unexpected, powerful re-emergence of national consciousness in the region conjured up the image of the 'Spring of Peoples' of 1848 for many experts. Many viewed the movements of political liberation and of national emancipation to be in close unity with one another, almost in a symbiotic relationship. In their perception, resurgent nationalism is a fundamentally positive phenomenon. It has a democratic and liberal content; it has been based on the fight to gain individual freedom and achieve popular sovereignty for its own community. The new states were constituted by the act of self-determination,

---

1. This chapter was written in 1997. For practical purposes, the term 'Central Europe' is used in this study to include that group of small and medium-size countries that were under Communist rule between the current borders of the European Union and the former Soviet Union. This does not include former Yugoslavia. International political science literature often uses the terms 'Central/Eastern Europe' and 'Central and South-eastern Europe' to denote the historical and cultural differences in the region itself. See, for instance, Samuel P. Huntington, 'The Clash of Civilizations?' *Foreign Affairs*, Vol. 72, No. 3, Summer 1993, pp. 29–31; Jeno Szucs, 'The Three Historical Regions of Europe: An Outline', *Acta Historica Academiae Scientarum Hungaricae*, Vol. 29, 1983, pp. 131–84. The academic debate on terminology and definition of the 'inner frontiers' of Europe continues.

opposing alien rule, a rule which had been considered illegitimate from the perspective of the (re)emerging democratic idea of popular sovereignty.[2]

On the other hand, another group of observers tends to portray nationalism as a pernicious force that spreads irrational behaviour, breeds fragmentation and leads inevitably to violent conflicts. This analysis reflects to a large extent a reaction to the unfolding drama in the former Yugoslavia and to the persecution of ethnic minorities in various countries of the region. Many believe that demonic forces are escaping as a Pandora's Box is being reopened,[3] and emphasize that after the disappearance of the 'ghost of Communism' (a reference made to the *Communist Manifesto,* also dating back to 1848), Western democracies have to face the appearance of a new one, this time the 'ghost of nationalism'.[4]

Supporters of both approaches, however, tend to agree on the strength of nationalism. The ethno-national renaissance of this decade has proved to be one of the most powerful factors shaping the history of the twentieth century. It has produced the most extensive geostrategic rearrangement of the European continent. The recent wave of national self-determination has fundamentally redrawn the map of Central and Eastern Europe, the Caucasus and former Soviet Central Asia, and resulted in a new configuration of powers in the post-Cold War world.

Self-determination, as it appeared in the early 1990s, was a liberating concept. Peoples who had been forced to live within the borders of countries with which they could not identify and whose regimes they detested profoundly, tried to free

2.   See, for instance, Ghia Nodia, 'Nationalism and Democracy', in Larry Diamond and Marc Plattner (eds.), *Nationalism, Ethnic Conflict and Democracy,* pp. 3–22, Baltimore/London, Johns Hopkins University Press, 1994; Nadia Diuk and Adrian Karatnycky, *New Nations Rising: The Fall of the Soviets and the Challenge of Independence,* pp. 21–40, New York, John Wiley, 1993. For a detailed analysis of the linkage between self-determination and popular sovereignty, see Walker Connor, *Ethnonationalism: The Quest for Understanding,* Princeton, Princeton University Press, 1994.

3.   See William T. Johnsen, *Pandora's Box Reopened: Ethnic Conflict in Europe and its Implications,* Carlisle Barrack, Pa., US Army War College, Strategic Studies Institute, 1994; Pauline H. Baker and John A. Ausink, 'State Collapse and Ethnic Violence: Toward a Predictive Model', *Parameters,* Vol. 26, No. 1, Spring 1996, pp. 19–31.

4.   See also Miroslav Hroch, 'National Self-determination from a Historical Perspective', in Sukumar Periwal (ed.), *Notions of Nationalism,* pp. 65–82, Budapest/London/New York, Central European University Publications, 1995.

New international 61
approaches to the solution
of ethnic problems in
Central Europe

themselves from this alien domination. Oppressed minorities sought emancipation for their language, culture and religion, and called for the right to participate more fully in decisions concerning their own community within the state. Throughout modern history, nationalism has all too often contained both defensive and offensive elements, constructive patriotic and destructive chauvinistic components. Often it was extremely difficult to separate these elements as the two tended to be totally intermingled in the history of individual nations. In Central Europe, throughout the last two centuries, oppressed nations, as soon as they obtained their own nation-state, began to persecute the minorities living on their territory in order to eliminate rival ethnic claims. In the process they used, more often than not, the same methods and ideological arguments as their former oppressors had used against their own claims.

The question of nationality has a long and complicated history in this region since the emergence of modern nations in the early nineteenth century. The post-Cold War resurgence of the ethnic and national questions has often been regarded as the simple reappearance of age-old, pre-World War conflict. It is our intention in this chapter to give an overview of various management efforts, policy instruments, legal and institutional techniques, which may facilitate successful accommodation of ethnic claims in consolidating the democratization process and the regional peace and stability in Central Europe.

NATIONALISM: 'OLD' AND 'NEW' FACETS

One of the most perennial features of the ethno-national phenomenon in the region is the separate development of statehood and nationhood. Traditionally, political and ethno-cultural borders have not coincided. Either the political entity, the state, was larger than the nation (comprising distinct ethno-national elements at the same time), or the 'nation' was spread out on a larger territory than that which belonged to the 'state' (which meant having kinship ties with minority groups in adjacent territories of neighbouring states).[5]

5.   See also Benjamin Akzin, *States and Nations*, New York, Anchor Books, 1966; Jaroslav Krejci and Vitezslav Velimsky, *Ethnic and Political Nations in Europe*, London, Croom Helm, 1981.

Historically, ethno-national minorities have been concentrated in the border regions geographically. Thus, once political frontiers shifted, the positions of political domination also shifted. These circumstances provide another important characteristic of Central European nationality problems which is fundamentally different from the general Western experience. In the United States, for instance, the problems of people belonging to minorities (primarily Afro-Americans and Hispano-Americans) have predominantly been considered human rights issues, a problem of equal opportunities. In Western Europe and Canada, on the other hand, minority populations demanded essentially cultural and territorial (regional) autonomy in the 1960s and 1980s. They received it in the form of a more decentralized or federal state. As opposed to these, in the post-Cold War era, Central and Eastern Europe have also treated the ethnic/nationality issue as an important factor of geopolitics.

Despite the obvious ethno-cultural diversity, the prevailing nation-state policy regards the state as the embodiment of a single nationality, as expressed for instance in the German *Staatsvolk* concept. Compared to the Western European historical development of nation-building, the nation-building efforts of many Central European countries came much too late. These efforts, from the perspective of the minority cultures within the newly forming nations, had involved inevitably nation-destroying elements as well, provoking various forms of resistance from the affected communities. In Central Europe, states tried to eliminate minorities and their culture by applying forcible assimilation policies throughout the twentieth century and cultural (or in the worst cases ethnic) cleansing, aside from rare and generally short-lived tolerant governmental practices.

The emotional or aggressive handling of ethnic problems created existential fears, and acted as a catalyst for a chain reaction in the communities, sometimes leading up to hysteria. These have tended to overshadow the more rational elements in the ongoing political debate on feasible multicultural accommodation. In a final analysis, they represented a serious obstacle to successful democratization and development of many countries of the region. Anti-minority (discriminatory or assimilationist) policies have historically tended to backfire.[6]

Several important new elements emerged in the reawakening of the ethno-national consciousness in Central Europe in the 1990s. The first might be its

New international 63
approaches to the solution
of ethnic problems in
Central Europe

unexpected intensity. This was magnified by several coinciding and overlapping crises in the region caused by the sudden and simultaneous disappearance of a political ideology and a regime, together with the disappearance of economic and military blocs.

These phenomena, combined with stagnant and declining living standards, high inflation and unemployment in several countries, enhanced the quest for smaller group identities. This, in turn, reinforced political alignments along ethnic lines and the drive towards a greater degree of political and cultural autonomy on societal or international level. The intensity of national consciousness also had a 'contagious' character, spreading as if by chain reaction. Successfully achieved ethno-national claims fuelled other attempts to have an independent state or a more decentralized state, allocating a greater degree of minority rights for the affected community. Media and the increased global and regional com-munications generally played an enormous role in intensifying the process.

Another major difference can be found in the reshaped international environment of the 1990s. The end of the bipolar confrontation has opened, at least potentially, a historically unprecedented opportunity for co-operation between great powers confronted all with new risks and threats of the post-Cold War era. There is no longer a willingness to return to the political realism of the inter-war era in Europe, when competing great powers took sides in the interstate and intrastate conflicts of Central Europe and the Balkans.

The effort to enhance the missions and mandate of the international organizations in the new era, as well as the emerging Western European integration process, played a crucial role in the change of individual state behaviour. Some states escalated into nationality conflicts with dramatic consequences: displacement of populations, suffering, huge loss of life and vast material destruction. These have also prompted a higher degree of readiness for co-operation among major international actors in order to contain ethnic-based hot wars and prevent the eruption of new ones.

---

6.   Istvan Bibo, 'The Distress of East-European Small States' in *Democracy, Revolution, Self-determination*, pp. 13–88, Highland Lakes, Atlantic Research and Publications, 1991; Donald L. Horowitz, 'Democracy in Divided Societies', in Diamond and Plattner, op. cit., pp. 35–55.

The crisis of European Communist states which led to their disappearance in the early 1990s coincided with the appearance of new thinking concerning the nation-state. As we approach the third millennium, the classic nineteenth-century concept of national sovereignty is declining. It is under a dual pressure, from inside and outside state borders. The traditional state structure is being challenged, both from below and from above. Deepening and enlarging regional integration, increasing global communications and multiplying cross-border contacts are weakening the states from above, whereas local communities, corporations and NGOs are taking over many former state functions.

This is not to say that the 'nation' is dying out in this process. No national interest has ceased to exist in the twentieth century. The nation-state will remain an enduring actor of international politics in the foreseeable future. It will continue to be the standard political organization. Predictions about a global collapse of states, despite the failures of state authority in several countries (Bosnia and Herzegovina, Somalia or Burundi), have been exaggerated.[7]

The trend caused by internal and external pressures on the state, and challenges from above and below, however, will probably lead to a more pronounced role of international organizations and a more powerful impact of international law on the behaviour of governmental and non-governmental actors alike.

It is almost paradoxical that several countries of Central Europe (and of the whole former Communist Europe and Asia) have gained or regained their independence at a time when the significance and the content of national sovereignty are under pressure to change. This contradiction can be resolved only by a modern interpretation of state sovereignty, one that rejects inward-looking and isolationist policies and is open to the ideas of international co-operation and integration. This attitude, if it gains ground, may facilitate international efforts to handle minority problems and prevent interethnic violence in the future.

---

7.   There are a number of studies based on this approach. See, for instance, Ralph Peters, 'The Culture of Future Conflict', *Parameters*, Vol. 25, No. 4, Winter 1995/96, pp. 18–27; Baker and Ausink, op. cit.

New international 65
approaches to the solution
of ethnic problems in
Central Europe

SECURITY THREATS: A POTENTIAL FOR ESCALATION INTO VIOLENCE?

There has been an in-depth discussion of Central and Eastern European ethnic tension in Western expert circles which has revealed an apparent discrepancy between Western political discussion and decisions. The message stemming from this discrepancy seemed anything but promising for the peaceful resolution of differences. At first, it seemed that unless tension had a direct impact on Western territory or interests, it was unlikely to provoke much more than academic interest there. Despite lengthy Western hesitancy concerning the war in former Yugoslavia, this perception has diminished since the Dayton Accord. For Western policy, the question is when and how ethnic tension escalates into violence.

Yet, even without becoming violent, ethnic discord has a potential to slow down, distort and ultimately impede the necessary economic and political reforms in Central and Eastern Europe. Thus, even when there is relatively little chance for ethnic tension to escalate, it is important to promote the peaceful democratic management of the conflict towards its gradual solution.

It is understandable that international interest in the post-Cold War outburst of national feeling in Central Europe has tended to focus on its potentially violent aspect. However, such an approach can develop into a unidimensional understanding of the problem. This does not promote the development of effective policies for dissolving ethnic tension. All aspects of Central European governmental policies should be examined closely. A balanced understanding of what has been achieved so far, based on how the countries of the region themselves dealt with the ethnic issue and with the tensions that sprang from it, helps us develop the right line of action for the future.

When the problem of ethnic minorities in Central Europe surfaced in 1989/90, the first deficiency in the manner of approaching it turned out to be the lack of standard international regulation. The issue of ethnic minorities is not specifically or exclusively a Central European problem but one that affects practically every state. Yet the international community had an unhappy experience with collective rights; the failure of the League of Nations is one reminder of this. Efforts to introduce universally accepted international norms in this field were further impeded by the reluctance of most Western European states to treat this problem in the framework of international law, for a variety of reasons. The goal of formalizing international standards of minority rights was tangible in some Central European governments' policies. It was undertaken through the Conference on Security and Co-operation in Europe (CSCE)[8] process, the Council of Europe and the various organs of the United Nations.[9]

While the frequent reference to the ethnic issue at international forums was often cited as a source of concern for Western countries, the rationale behind establishing international standards on potentially contentious issues is a proof in itself of the democratic intentions of Central European governments. Many newly elected Central European policy-makers believed that the most effective way of handling the question of minority rights was by developing an internationally accepted and respected code of conduct for treating minorities, by 'denationalizing' the conflict.

In addition to their policy efforts in international legal forums, Central European countries were the major initiators of regional co-operation in 1989/90. The Visegrad co-operation was launched as well as the Pentagonale, which later developed into the Hexagonale and ultimately the Central European Initiative (CEI), as well as the establishment of the Central European Free Trade Area (CEFTA). Although it was understood from the very beginning that regional co-operation is at best an indirect and long-term policy tool for solving the problem of ethnic minorities in the region, it was expected that a web of relations among these countries would ultimately contribute to the stability of intraregional relations over time. While regional co-operation could not develop to its full potential for a number of reasons, continued efforts through the slow but noticeable regional dialogue were a signal for the peaceful resolution of conflicts.

Tensions surrounding the presence of ethnic minorities and the issue of collective minority rights touched upon multiple sensitivities in most Western

8.   Now the Organization for Security and Co-operation in Europe (OSCE).
9.   On the establishing of European norms by Western democracies since the end of the Cold War, see also George Schopflin, 'Nationalism and Ethnic Minorities in Post-Communist Europe', in Richard Kaplan and John Feffer (eds.), *Europe's New Nationalism, States and Minorities in Conflict*, pp. 151–68, New York/Oxford, Oxford University Press, 1996.

New international 67
approaches to the solution
of ethnic problems in
Central Europe

European countries. It was a problematic question in bilateral relations of neighbouring Central European countries, especially lacking internationally accepted norms, and was further complicated by the linkage established by some between the treatment of minorities and the respect for national borders. It is of great interest to understand whether and, if so, how Central European policies contributed to the development of peaceful conflict management and to the stabilization of the region, or whether the policies have tended to increase the potential of military escalation of the nationality conflict.

A close analysis of the fields of bilateral relations in Central Europe shows an important difference between those concerned with diplomatic-political relations and those concerned with military diplomacy. Contrary to the relations between ministries of foreign affairs, those between neighbouring ministries of defence have been significantly and consistently better.

As evidenced by policies of neighbouring Central European governments, there has been a detectable and continued effort to keep disagreements on the cultural, human rights and political levels, and not to let them escalate into the field of military diplomacy.[10] A quick overview of relations in the field of defence among the countries generally regarded to have the most tense relations reveals that, even in the first few years of the post-Cold War era, at a time when nationalism-related tensions were high in Central Europe, actual bilateral military relations were stable and positive. The May 1991 'Open Skies Agreement' between Romania and Hungary, together with various other security-related agreements, the numerous meetings, the undisturbed support for the Conventional Forces in Europe (CFE) spirit, the October 1993 Slovak–Hungarian agreement on an immediate consultation mechanism, as well as their July 1994 declaration to disregard accidental violations of their respective airspace during training flights, and numerous other decisions all prove that the tensions surrounding the situation of the ethnic minorities have been most consciously and carefully kept out of the military domain. Ethnic/nationality conflict in Central

---

10.   For an excellent analysis of the arising (political, demographic, cultural, economic, social and psychological) alienation of the ethnic groups within a society lacking in policies targeted at the various fields, see Guy Heraud, *Les Communautés linguistiques en quête d'un statut*, pp. 22–30, Nice, Presses d'Europe, 1990.

Europe, used for political and rhetorical purposes is, and has been since 1989, cultural, historical and political in nature, but not military.

Therefore the prime focus of international effort has to shift to removing the psychological fears that exist in some Central European countries. This may seem but a small difference in historical perspectives: examples abound of wars that were launched out of psychological fears. The difference is far more important, however, if our goal is to develop effective policies to solve the problem arising from nationalism. If our analysis on the socio-psychological character of these old/new problems holds, a great deal of effort has to focus on socio-psychological measures.

The emergence of nationalism in parallel to the end of Communism was seen by some as the coming out of deep freeze of ancient memories and long-buried feelings. For others, it was the 'revenge' of nationalism that was able to put an end to Communist internationalism.[11] Either way, without the cohesive force of nationalism, the revolutions of 1989/90 would probably not have come about. The attainment of national sovereignty is the most important development in national history. It is not surprising that such a powerful force needed to be expressed also in the diverse aspects of the new democracies' policies.

Yet national feelings were not the exclusive influential aspiration after the attainment of national independence. Equally important was the desire to reincorporate the European idea. It is needless to enumerate the many examples of the Central European self-identification with, and the incorporation of, the European idea.[12] These two together, and in their interaction, constituted the basis of various policies in practically all Central European countries. Both of these aspirations were further enhanced by these countries' experience of having their normal historical development brutally interrupted by Soviet aggression.[13]

11. On the negative force of nationalism, see also Misha Glenny, *The Rebirth of History, Eastern Europe in the Age of Democracy*, London, Penguin Books, 1990, 1993.

12. Thomas W. Simmons Jr, *Eastern Europe in the Postwar World*, pp. 226–67, New York, St Martin's Press, 1993, offers a good insight into the many parallel forces after the end of the Cold War.

13. On the strength of the idea of 'returning to Europe', see Andrew Cottey, *East-Central Europe after the Cold War, Poland, the Czech Republic, Slovakia and Hungary in Search of Security*, London, Macmillan Press, 1995.

New international 69
approaches to the solution
of ethnic problems in
Central Europe

It is the effort to conciliate and harmonize these two driving forces that offers the most balanced basis of analysis of this area's nationality policies throughout the period. It can be argued that the European idea has increasingly inspired decisions in Central Europe, from the economic field through the cultural to the political, and that has influenced measuring the failure of reforms as well.

At the same time, it is the power of the European idea that gives us the clearest indication to the trend that ethnic tensions are not likely to lead to military confrontation in the future either. While tensions (ethnic, among others) escalated militarily in the former Soviet Union or the Balkans, developments do not lead the careful observer to draw parallels between these events and those in Central Europe. Central European countries have demonstrated altogether different conflict-managing techniques and mechanisms.

The fact that the primary goal of all of these countries is to integrate into the Western world has had a tangible and empirically verifiable impact on their ways of conflict management, if not yet conflict 'resolution'. In tackling the problems that characterize the entire region, they followed Western approaches and methods. They have shown that they have learnt from the democratic ideals in their practical decision-making. This fundamental strength of the European idea plays a key role in developing further steps to solve the remaining ethnic tension in Central Europe.

The power of Western European thinking in conflict management has been enough to avoid the militarization of ethnic tensions in Central Europe, but managing a conflict, however peacefully, does not amount to solving it. Dissatisfaction by ethnic minorities remains a characteristic of certain countries of the region and threatens to linger on over an extended period of time, unless the international community undertakes policy measures to promote their ultimate solution in a peaceful environment. What is essential is to deal with the root causes of ethnic conflicts.

MULTICULTURALISM: A NEW PARADIGM IN INTERETHNIC RELATIONS

The more than four decades of the Cold War division of the continent and especially of the Pax Sovietica in the Eastern part transformed this historically troubled region into a peaceful one. However, the cost of this stability, which included the loss of political freedom and national independence, was considerable. After the fall of the Iron Curtain, Central Europe needs more than ever a new paradigm in international policy, which implies also a change of mentality in domestic political processes. The previous authoritarian methods of maintaining stability by containment and coercion could not be successful in the long run and cannot be brought back after the dismantling of the Warsaw Pact. For an accommodation of ethnic claims to be effective, it must be based on the political conviction that there is no alternative to peaceful coexistence of majorities and minorities.

Events of recent years have disproved the apocalyptic predictions of a chaos of small states and of tribal wars encompassing the whole, or a large part, of the region.[14] Armed conflicts between nationalities (ethnic communities) that erupted in the former Yugoslavia and in some regions of the former Soviet Union sent a clear message that Central and Eastern Europe might be just another potential area of conflict and seismic movements. Reality provides empirical evidence to the contrary, but such a broad generalization calls for at least two further reservations. On the one hand, there are wide differences between countries of Central and Eastern Europe and the former Soviet Union, including their ethnic composition and minority policies. In the geographical arc from the Baltic to the Adriatic and the Black Sea, the political weight of the nationality issue is generally greater in the south-eastern countries than in the countries to their north and west. In terms of ethnic composition the following countries have relatively few minorities on their territory, constituting 2 to 4 per cent of the total population: Poland (Germans, Ukrainians, Czechs); the Czech Republic (gypsies or Roma, Germans, Poles, Slovaks); Hungary (Germans, gypsies, Slovaks, Romanians); Slovenia (Italians, Hungarians) and Albania (Greeks). Another group of states: Slovakia (Hungarians, gypsies, Ukrainians, Czechs); Romania (Hungarians, gypsies, Germans, Serbs) and Bulgaria (Turks, gypsies) has a larger minority population. Their ratio exceeds 10 to 15 per cent of the total population; in some districts and

---

14.   See, for instance, François Thual, *Les conflits identitaires*, Paris, Éditions Ellipses, 1994; John J. Mearshimer, 'Back to the Future: Instability in Europe after the Cold War', *International Security*, Vol. 15, No. 1, Summer 1990, pp. 5–56.

**New international
approaches to the solution
of ethnic problems in
Central Europe**   71

areas their percentage constitutes an absolute majority. The minority population of the Baltic states is even more important, both in terms of their ratio and of their domestic political significance (in Latvia, for instance, ethnic Russians constitute almost half of the total population).[15] Obviously, the more the population of a country is composed of multinational and multicultural entities, the more complex this issue becomes.

Lower figures, however, do not necessarily indicate smaller political problems. A small percentage of minorities in a state in and by itself does not guarantee a lack of ethnicity-related tension. Nevertheless, we must keep in mind that recent changes in the international environment have also opened new opportunities for prevention and management, when judging the magnitude of today's risks.

There is no compelling historical evidence that nationality tensions inevitably escalate into violent conflict and tribal wars. Societal disasters of these kinds can be anticipated, prevented or at least moderated by domestic and international measures. Policies directed at the root causes of ethnic tension have proved to be effective in improving the situation in many countries of the world.

When facing the challenge of how best to accommodate multiculturalism, both states and minorities in Central Europe often suffer from an 'insecurity complex'. States fear isolationist or separatist tendencies among the minorities. They often tend to analyse their situation by thinking of it as a slippery slope and believing that even a modest request by the minority, if accepted by the majority, might start an avalanche: a small gesture today will result in a disaster tomorrow; an elementary school in the mother tongue of a minority today, a loss of territory tomorrow. Minorities also fear that they might become the target of forced assimilation or, even worse, of ethnic cleansing at any time. As they were frequently victims of state-sponsored nationalism in the Communist past, the memory of recent pain breeds and maintains mistrust towards authority and a permanent suspicion concerning the underlying intentions of the majority government. Sometimes these concerns are based on concrete historical

15.   For ethno-demographic census data, see *World Directory of Minorities, Minority Rights Group's Edition*, London, Longman International Reference, 1990.

experiences, sometimes on unfounded perceptions. But whatever the basis, these problems need to be treated with great sensitivity.

There are democratic institutional and procedural methods that may stabilize both the position of states and the domestic status of minorities. These methods promote minority integration – not assimilation – into the society. It is only in this way that the general civic identity of the state can be developed and the minorities' own ethnic identity preserved at the same time. In other words, loyalty to the state in which they live and of which they are citizens does not prohibit or contradict the minorities' right to preserve and develop their own national and ethnic characteristics. Rather, they go hand in hand.

These two elements are in contradiction only for those who define the nation-state as a homogenized, over-centralized mono-ethnic entity. They may be inclined to reject concepts such as multiculturalism, ethnic pluralism, multinational federation, autonomy or minority protection, and to support the concepts of assimilation and/or emigration of the minority(ies) as a realistic means of achieving a homogeneous nation-state and of solving the ethnic problem.

Such assimilationist thinking is not a new concept in Central and Eastern Europe. Its ideological roots go back to the late nineteenth century. Compared with the frequent ethnic strife of the pre-war period, the Communist system did very little to change effectively the relations between nations and ethnic groups in the area, despite its 'internationalist' rhetoric.[16] The Communist regimes, far from solving the tensions, froze them. The propaganda discourse on the rapprochement and merging of socialist nations and nationalities (*sblizhenie i slianie,* in the Soviet political dictionary) covered the policies of forcible assimilation and subordination to the interests of the dominant nations.

It is pertinent to highlight the Western experiences in solving minority problems during the Cold War. The long-lasting Flemish–Walloon conflict in Belgium is well known. Departing from its inter-community tensions, Belgium has developed an innovative constitutional arrangement for multicultural

16.   An interesting collection of the reflections of the political actors in the Communist and post-Communist periods can be found in Gale Stokes, *From Stalinism to Pluralism, A Documentary History of Eastern Europe since 1945,* New York, Oxford University Press, 1996 (on 'Nationalism', see pp. 257–72).

New international   73
approaches to the solution
of ethnic problems in
Central Europe

accommodation combining territorial and linguistic criteria. It is not without problems even today, but the legal and political efforts to find solutions for ethnic coexistence are worthy of attention. The Spanish experience is equally important. Spain undertook a major reform of decentralization of government in the 1970s, after General Franco's death. In this process, the ethnic communities, primarily the Catalans and the Basques, re-established their autonomy.

The 'devolution' in the United Kingdom reinforced self-rule in Wales and Scotland. No similar solution has been possible in Northern Ireland so far. There, intercommunal strife has not yet found a settlement, despite renewed domestic and international efforts. In Italy, Alto Adige, Tyrol, was a place of violent interethnic conflict in the 1950s. Today the German-speaking minority of this region enjoys significant cultural autonomy, which is also reinforced by interstate co-operation between Austria and Italy. This co-operation is similar to the cultural exchange between ethnic Danes and Germans in the Schleswig region, across the German–Danish frontier. The Swedish-speaking population of Finland, 8 per cent of the total population, also enjoys the advantages of Nordic regional co-operation. This minority was accorded large cultural autonomy combined with territorial autonomy for the Swedish inhabitants of the Åland Islands. The Swiss model of multiculturalism and multilingualism, based on the cantonal system, goes back to the Middle Ages. It officially recognizes the equal cultural rights of the German-, French- and Italian-speaking communities. The Swiss Confederation also promotes the minority rights of a 40,000-strong community, called Romansch or Raeto-romans. Their language is officially used in the canton where they live, Grisons, and it is recognized as one of the four national languages on the level of the Confederation in Switzerland.[17]

Emerging Western European integration and Nordic regional co-operation also made a significant impact on the perception and the norms of how democratic nations can and should live side by side. Political frontiers ceased being dividing lines between peoples and started gradually to disappear within the European Community, now the European Union. Exchanges at the grass-roots

17. John Coakley (ed.), *The Territorial Management of Ethnic Conflict*, London, Frank Cass, 1993; Joseph V. Montville, *Conflict and Peacemaking in Multiethnic Societies*, pp. 131–238, Lexington, Mass., Lexington Books/D.C. Heath, 1991.

level between individuals, institutions, smaller or larger communities, have become a mass phenomenon. Policies including youth exchange or the twin-city movement have been set up to improve relations between nations with difficult historical legacy, for example the French and the Germans in Western Europe and the Danes and Norwegians in the Nordic region.

There was no similar undertaking in the historically sensitive relationships in Eastern Europe during the Cold War. The Polish–Lithuanian, Czech–German, Slovak–Ukrainian, Hungarian–Romanian, Romanian–Ukrainian and Romanian–Russian, Bulgarian–Serbian, Serbian–Albanian relationships were all 'frozen'. Until very recent times, East European societies remained essentially closed to one another. This situation more often than not preserved the old national stereotypes and the distorted clichés about other nations. Also, there was a widening gap between the official discourse of 'fraternal friendship' and political reality. In the 1970s when Spain, Belgium, France and the United Kingdom undertook a fundamental territorial decentralization, giving more power to their respective regions and to the nationalities living there, the central power of the state was reinforced in Czechoslovakia, Romania, Yugoslavia and the Soviet Union.

Despite widespread scepticism, the minority problem has become an important issue of debate in the domestic democratization process. It has been widely recognized that democracy in Central Europe cannot be stable without a fair treatment of the minority issue.

INTERETHNIC RELATIONS: FACING THE CHALLENGE

A brief overview of the principal legal instruments developed in this decade is of interest. The pressure of ongoing events has made it clear that the nationality issue has increasingly become a pre-eminent problem to deal with. As a result, a number of normative instruments have come into being. Already, the 1990 Copenhagen meeting of the CSCE in its final document supported 'affirmative action' in favour of minority rights. The same year, Recommendation No. 1134 adopted by the Parliamentary Assembly of the Council of Europe addressed the issue of the rights of minorities. In December 1992, the United Nations General Assembly adopted the Declaration on the Rights of Persons Belonging to

New international
approaches to the solution
of ethnic problems in
Central Europe   75

National, Ethnic, Religious or Linguistic Minorities. Since the end of the Second World War, this Declaration is the first document dealing exclusively with the problem of persons belonging to minorities that has a universal character. This fact also indicates the substantial resistance to progress in the international codification of minority rights for many decades. Several major decisions followed. At its Helsinki summit meeting in 1992, the CSCE took a highly innovative step in deciding on the creation of the Office of the High Commissioner on National Minorities. The High Commissioner, with a team of experts, regularly monitors the implementation of minority rights in the OSCE (formerly the CSCE) member states, especially in Central and Eastern Europe. The Council of Europe also showed an increased interest in relation to minority issues. In 1993 the Council adopted the Vienna Declaration, the annex of which relates to minorities. The same year in Strasbourg, the Parliamentary Assembly of the Council of Europe adopted Recommendation No. 1201 regarding the rights of national minorities, an Additional Protocol on the Rights of National Minorities.[18]

Among other initiatives, mention should also be made of the Charter of Paris for a New Europe, signed in Paris in 1990, which contains articles concerning minorities. The Stability Pact of 1994 also focused on the two pillars of regional security and good-neighbourly relations in Central Europe. It underlined the inviolability of the existing state borders and the respect for the rights of minorities living in their territories.

In accordance with the Stability Pact, most Central European countries also signed bilateral treaties and agreements which include stipulations concerning the borders and the treatment of minorities. Poland signed such a document with all its neighbours; Hungary signed a basic treaty (or agreement promoting minority rights) with Ukraine, Slovenia, Croatia and more recently with Slovakia and Romania.

The test of these bilateral agreements is, obviously, their implementation. These documents should not be seen as an end but, rather, as the beginning of a process. They can be crucial instruments for the consolidation of security in the

---

18.   An interesting analysis can be found in Timothy D. Sisk, *Power Sharing and International Mediation in Ethnic Conflict*, Washington, D.C., Carnegie Commission, 1996 (US Institute of Peace, 'Perspectives' Series).

area, if they bring about actual co-operation in interstate relations, and if they improve the status of minorities inside the countries.

The adoption of universal and regional instruments concerning minority protection demonstrates that real progress has been made since 1990 with respect to ethnic problems. However, it must also be emphasized that international norms represent the minimum standard of minority protection. The domestic political practice of several democratic countries goes far beyond these minimum requirements and offers more advantageous conditions for minorities than those defined in universal or regional documents, as the examples of some Western European states showed. As a whole, however, increased international discussions prove that the treatment of minorities is no longer an exclusively internal affair, and that the 'external' interest of the international community is a legitimate one. This is an important step forward in the evolution of human rights as well as in the development of the international system.

Institutional plurality provides an answer to diversity of ethnic and national cultures in a society. There are various forms of culturally pluralist policy, in which language and education are issues that enjoy priority generally. As language plays a key role in national identity, the protection of the mother tongue is one of the most important 'survival strategies' of minorities. Depending on the country's ethnic composition, either aspiration for state bilingualism or for local bilingualism can be found (the latter describes the official use of two languages in administrative districts where minorities constitute the majority of the local population). Institutional plurality also can help minorities to claim their right for their own educational and cultural institutions enabling them to preserve and develop their identity and cultural uniqueness within society.

Participation and power-sharing – by taking part in central or local government coalitions – might also be essential. For instance, one of the Hungarian parties participated in the Slovak coalition government between 1992 and 1994; and in the same period the party of the Turkish minority participated in the Bulgarian central government. In Romania, national minorities participate in running local administrations in areas of their geographic concentration. After the November 1996 national elections, which brought centrist/centre-right parties into power, the Democratic Alliance of Hungarians in Romania (RMDSZ) also

New international 77
approaches to the solution
of ethnic problems in
Central Europe

accepted ministerial responsibilities in the new cabinet formed in December 1996 in Bucharest. In Slovenia and Hungary, where the ratio of minorities is lower, original forms of participatory rights in local administrations have been developed to satisfy the autonomy aspirations of these groups.

The territorial management of ethnic conflicts, the subdivision of the state into smaller administrative units better to assure minority self-government may also be an effective technique to ease tensions between nationalities.[19] Whether the political elite of the dominant community and the central government want to create such a decentralized government is of course a different matter. In Central Europe, even in recent years, we can also see some opposing political efforts, such as the ethnic policing of the territorial units to give the dominant nationality numerical preponderance even in geographic areas of minority concentration. Home rule based on local municipal, county or regional (provincial) level as well as federal or confederate solutions to accommodate ethnic claims offer serious chances that the worst of the tensions may be allayed and the nationalities find satisfaction in coexistence with other communities within an integrated society.

Education and media could play an outstanding role in changing attitudes, promoting values of tolerance and understanding in interethnic relations. There have been a few positive initiatives in this field. National expert committees were established to reconcile critical aspects of history textbooks used in public education, improving the accuracy of historical interpretations on both sides. Domestic and international private teaching institutions are setting up programmes promoting civic values of tolerance, countering in this way nationalist propaganda, which is sometimes still heavily present in the state-run education systems of certain societies. Emerging modern technologies of communication, the revolutionary changes in transmission and processing of information, including satellite TV broadcasts and global information highways,

---

19. For an international overview of minority rights and their institutional accommodation, see *The Situation of Minorities in Europe* (Political Series W-4), Strasbourg, European Parliament, 1993; Georg Brunner, *Nationalitatenprobleme und Minderheitenkonflikte in Osteuropa*, Gütersloh, Verlag Bertelsmann Stiftung, 1996. On the role of the High Commissioner on National Minorities, see Diane Chigas, 'Bridging the Gap between Theory and Practice: The CSCE High Commissioner on National Minorities', *Helsinki Monitor*, No. 3, 1994, pp. 27–41.

have also introduced new technical means and opportunities to enhance chances of decentralized, multicentric, interacting Central European societies, where the minority values and interests might be better articulated. Yet, despite actual progress, realism commands conservative optimism: compared to the needs of societies, the programmes promoting tolerance and a culture of peace are still few in number and modest in their societal spill-over. More should be done, especially since the dominant type of conflict in current world politics, and probably in the period ahead, is internal conflict, which has, in most cases, roots in ethnic and cultural policies. By the shift of focus from interstate to intrastate confrontation, the significance of the cultural aspects of security has been dramatically increased.

Successful coexistence is not possible between national majorities and minorities without widening the political horizons of these communities. When the universal and regional (including European and transatlantic) institutions project their values and ideals in this part of Europe, they widen the range of examples and create a larger area of shared values and codes of conduct. This has the potential eventually to develop a common security identity on the continent, to encourage subregional co-operation, and to enhance the transparency, the 'crossability' of state boundaries. A large number of political and security challenges have become international in scope, such as environmental problems, organized crime, terrorism, uncontrolled migration. It is no longer possible for an individual state to manage these by relying exclusively on its own resources. Future extension of West European and Euro-Atlantic institutions can provide a favourable multilateral framework for the management of bilateral ethnic discord. As both the European Union's and NATO's experience proves, integration multiplies forums for communication and increases the number of diplomatic, political and military channels for early warning and crisis management.

Subregional co-operation can also create a larger geographical and political setting beneficial for successful accommodation of minority claims. The state-centred, isolationist tendency of the Warsaw Pact/COMECON period has already been mentioned. With the collapse of Communism and its international system – albeit not without compromises and setbacks – we are witnessing a modest opening: the revival of a few subregional and interregional forms of co-

New international   79
approaches to the solution
of ethnic problems in
Central Europe

operation in Central Europe, such as the Central European Initiative, the Alpe-Adria, or Carpathian co-operation.

These frameworks are considered as complementary and not substitutes for the Western integration of this region. By multiplying cross-border contacts of individuals, local communities and enterprises, they contribute to better economic performance of participants and enhance values of civic society after decades of subordination of persons and groups to all-powerful state power. As the positive examples of the Slovenian–Hungarian–Austrian and the Czech–Polish (Cieszyn) border area demonstrate, subregional co-operation in territories of mixed ethnicity might also help national minorities to increase their cultural exchanges across the border.

As in the case for some other regions, Central Europe needs more programmes and action in order to enable its civic societies to raise the level of political culture, to increase understanding in majority/minority relations. In these countries, confidence-building in intercommunity relations means to encourage co-operative and discourage confrontational behaviour; promote the involvement of various ethnic groups in joint problem-solving; develop the capacity to understand the other side's position and enhance the capability of compromise in the political bargaining process. These efforts may help dispel suspicions, held by part of the majority population, which prompt people to discover in every minority endeavour some anti-state intent that endangers the country's sovereignty or territorial integrity. Mutual confidence-building can create a new atmosphere, what a minority and human rights expert called 'minority friendly environment' (*minderheitsfreundliche Umwelt*).[20] From the minority perspective, the contribution of international organizations and NGOs can dispel feelings of abandonment and hopelessness, which have already pressed these communities (or some of their representatives) a number of times in the direction of seeking irrational, violent solutions to their problems.

The significance of minority problems in Central Europe will not decrease, but rather increase in the period ahead. Events of recent years have demonstrated that multiethnicity has to be accommodated. Because of the political weight of

20. Felix Ermacora, Austrian human rights expert.

multiethnicity in Central Europe, success or failure in this domain will be relevant
to the entire region's political environment. The way in which issues related to
minorities are treated by political actors, will influence substantially the future of
peace and stability in the area as well as the chances of democracy in the
individual countries of the region.

Multinational efforts targeted at offering better psychological background for
the discussion of ethnic problems are worth mentioning. The methods include the
setting up of minority round tables and inter-community councils (the latter have
proved their beneficial impact on Protestant–Catholic co-operation under the
auspices of local authorities in Northern Ireland for instance),[21] foundations and
think tanks established by non-governmental organizations to encourage dialogue.
The Carnegie Foundation's Project on Ethnic Relations, for instance, established
unofficial, informal meetings between politicians and public figures belonging to
the Hungarian community in Romania and Romanian politicians. The German
Bertelsmann Foundation has also initiated similar forums for dialogue between
representatives of the Slovakian majority and the Hungarian minority in Slovakia.

CONCLUSION

Central and Eastern European countries might find it useful to observe the
manner in which the Western democracies have dealt with their ethnic problems.
They might draw on the successes and failures of these experiences, in their
positive as well as negative aspects.[22] Western European models were developed
in specific historical and societal circumstances; consequently they cannot and
should not be automatically copied. However, it should be noted that Western
political and economic arrangements can offer useful insights for Central Europe.
They testify that democratic and effective legal and political solutions of ethnic coexistence are indeed in the realm of the possible. These models, together with the
new instruments for international protection of minorities, contain numerous

21.   Colin Knox and Joanne Hughes, 'Community Relations in Northern Ireland', *Journal of
      Peace Research*, No. 1, 1996, pp. 83–98.
22.   Lucas, Lord Chilworth, *National Minorities in Central and Eastern Europe*, p. 13, Brussels,
      North Atlantic Assembly, Civilian Affairs Committee (Reports), 1992.

New international 81
approaches to the solution
of ethnic problems in
Central Europe

normative and institutional elements which can also be incorporated in the developing minority policies of the Central European states.

Ethnic diversity is a global phenomenon and it will remain a part of modern, pluralist world civilization in the foreseeable future. The UNESCO World Conference on Cultural Policies held in Mexico City in 1982 stated in its Final Report:

Every culture represents a unique and irreplaceable body of values since each people's traditions and forms of expression are its most effective means of demonstrating its presence in the world. The assertion of cultural identity therefore contributes to the liberation of peoples. Conversely, any form of domination constitutes a denial or an impairment of that identity.[23]

Special characteristics do not hinder but enrich the community of universal values uniting peoples. Hence recognition of the presence of variety of cultural identities whenever various traditions exist side by side constitutes the very essence of cultural pluralism.

There is an inclination to see ethnic identity as a source of trouble and minorities as potential trouble-makers. This indicates a reversal in the relation between causes and consequences; it is not ethnic diversity in and of itself, but the perception and treatment of it, that constitute the roots of conflicts. Nationalistic and exclusivist policies directed against minorities can be highly destabilizing and may ultimately lead to violence. Promotion of minority rights and multicultural policies can reduce aggressive strains of chauvinism in both majority and minority.

At the end of the twentieth century minority questions cannot be solved with the political 'methods' practised by irredentist movements, by forcible border changes, ethnic cleansing or massive deportations. Nor is the 'cultural ethnic cleansing', the forced assimilation of minorities, an acceptable method for civilized societies. Today, when distinct ethnic and national communities number in the thousands, whereas there are only some 180 states, forcible homogenization and political subordination cannot be an answer to the problem of multiculturalism.

23. World Conference on Cultural Policies, *Final Report*, UNESCO, Mexico City, 26 July–6 August 1982, pp. 41–2.

The more the minority sees its own interests and values respected, the less likely it is to embrace radicalism and extremism. Tolerance by the majority towards the minority's autonomy tends to strengthen a common civic identity. If national minorities have the right to cultivate their own identity in the state they live in, they tend to develop more respect for the territorial integrity of their country and for the rule of law there. As a collection of essays dedicated to the ethnic and national problems in contemporary Europe concludes:

The experience of Western Europe strongly suggests that accommodating calls for increased protection of minorities satisfies rather than fuels separatist tendencies. Across Western Europe, minority groups that enjoy a substantial degree of cultural freedom live comfortably inside states dominated by other ethnic groups.[24]

A 1992 report of the North Atlantic Assembly Civilian Affairs Committee makes a similar concluding proposal for the Central European countries.

Genuine motivation for entering into political compromise in Central European countries is often hard to find. Compromise is often viewed as a sign of weakness and not as part and parcel of the political decision-making process. It is thus not an overstatement to say that minority problems tend to be a true indication of ongoing troubles of general domestic political life in Central Europe. They are rooted in the intellectual and institutional disposition of the governing elite or of the general population towards cultural differences.

Most tensions due to the relation between majorities and minorities in Central Europe carry the burden of historical prejudices, negative stereotypes and mutual suspicion about true intentions. In such a heavily loaded environment, policies need to be targeted at the socio-psychological level as well. Without these, economic, bilateral political or other measures cannot effectively defuse mutual hatred. These psychological efforts imply influencing group beliefs and attitudes in favourable directions, and creating and maintaining a readiness on the part of communities living together to engage in dialogue.

---

24.   See also Charles A. Kupchan (ed.), *Nationalism and Nationalities in the New Europe*, p. 187, Ithaca/London, Cornell University Press, 1995.

New international 83
approaches to the solution
of ethnic problems in
Central Europe

There is a noteworthy relationship between minority policy and democracy. The political treatment of minorities credibly mirrors the general political culture prevailing in a society. This in turn affects the situation of the national majorities. On the other hand, especially within countries that have a substantial minority population and that are going through fundamental political changes, minority policy can become the Archimedean point of democracy, a relatively small device which can move the complex machinery of general democratic political construction.

Tolerant multicultural policies may have a beneficial spill-over effect on the democratization process of societies in transition as a whole. Ethnic, pluralist and political integrationist currents have proved not to be mutually exclusive in the experience of established democracies. They act simultaneously upon individuals and groups within the same society, contributing to the development of multiple and overlapping identities of the modern world. The diverse nationalities can become a moderating factor for inducing political stability within and between states in Central Europe.

The role of confidence-building measures in the prevention and resolution of conflicts

Wojciech Multan

THE SCOPE AND NATURE OF CONFIDENCE-BUILDING MEASURES – AN OUTLINE OF THEIR EVOLUTION

At the outset it should be acknowledged that the term 'confidence-building measures'[1] is among the least precisely defined in the field of international relations. This situation continues notwithstanding the vast research that has gone on in this field and the progress that has been made in the last quarter of a century.[2] However, no publication contains a thorough and precise definition of the term. The most important reason for this shortcoming is the virtually unlimited variety of actions, solutions and agreements which are regarded as

1. Treated here as synonyms for the concepts: 'confidence-building measures' (CBMs) and 'confidence- and security-building measures' (CSBMs).
2. Among numerous publications discussing this question, the following should be mentioned: J. Macintosh, 'Confidence-Building Measures. A Conceptual Exploration', in R. B. Byers, F. S. Larrabee and A. Lynch (eds), *Confidence-Building Measures and International Security*, pp. 9–29, New York, Institute for East–West Security Studies, 1983; K. Birnbaum (ed.), *Confidence-Building and East–West Relations*, Laxenburg, 1982; R. Berg and A. D. Rotfeld (eds.), *Building Security in Europe. Confidence-Building Measures and CSCE*, New York, Institute for East–West Security Studies, 1986; K. Kaiser (ed.), *Confidence-Building Measures*, Forschungsinstitut der Deutschen Gesellschaft für Auswartige Politik E.V., 1983; J. J. Holst, 'Confidence-Building Measures. A Conceptual Framework', *Survival*, Vol. 25, No. 1, 1983; N. Chadha, 'Confidence-Building Measures: A Theoretical Framework', in H. Gunter Brauch (ed.), *Confidence-Building. Verification and Conversion*, Mosbach, 1993 (Afes Press Report No. 39).

confidence-building in international relations. Moreover, on the one hand we have to deal with an enormous number of objective facts, events and processes making up present reality and, on the other hand, with a perception of these facts, events and processes that does not always faithfully reflect this reality. Confidence-building measures are supposed to apply to both the reality and its perception. Our knowledge about what these measures are is still incomplete, and it is practice rather than more or less abstract theoretical investigations that will gradually reveal all the features of this concept.

My purpose is not to engage in a wide-ranging discussion on the definition of these measures, but only to show that the situation does not improve with the passage of time, because these measures are being expanded at a pace that outstrips research in this field. Besides this, resolutions are being put into practice which – despite the fact that they are not confidence-building measures – in fact perform such a role.

It is commonly believed that confidence-building measures 'have a role to play in almost every situation where two or more parties are at loggerheads with each other'.[3] The need to employ such measures intensifies especially 'when two adversaries have a negative assessment of the perceived intentions and capabilities for each other which may be due to their incompatibility of goals or misperceptions and mistrust or both and yet want to establish a better working relationship'.[4] The confidence-building process starts when at least one – or both – of the adversaries become aware of the need to reach agreement. They may also serve as useful tools to prevent differences of interests between states/large social groups – irrespective of the sources of these differences – from reaching a critical point, such as the threat to use force or the use of force. Thus they constitute a kind of alternative to mistrust and tensions between two adversaries by the proposal to establish relations of a co-operative nature between them. Hence this is a strategy 'to promote détente, meaning relaxation of tension between the adversaries by mitigating mistrust and clarifying misperceptions'.[5]

---

3.   Cf. Chadha, op. cit., pp. 9–35.
4.   Ibid.
5.   Ibid.

The role of confidence-
building measures
in the prevention and
resolution of conflicts

87

The genesis of confidence-building measures, a phenomenon understood as a certain set of actions, procedures and mechanisms to prevent armed conflicts in relations between states – and, if despite these measures such conflicts do arise, to control and settle them – is connected with the military aspects of these relations. 'In theory, confidence- and security-building measures (CSBMs) assume that clarifying military intentions and capabilities will help to prevent conflict from emerging in the first place'.[6] In time, this concept gradually has been applied to other aspects of relations between states and even to relations between large social groups whose extreme behaviours could have certain international implications. This means that these measures could also be applied to various conflicts in a state's external and domestic policy, to political, social, nationality, ethnic, cultural and other questions. It is of little importance whether behind the dispute – a potential conflict with the use of force – lies a real difference of interests of the parties or only a difference of their perception.

The vast majority of people associate confidence-building measures with the Conference on Security and Co-operation in Europe (CSCE)[7] and the Helsinki Final Act signed at the conclusion of the conference (1975). However, the more inquisitive search for the archetype of confidence- and security-building measures in the remote past, recalling descriptions of the Peloponnese War.[8] Others call our attention to the period between the First and Second World Wars and to the years of the Cold War after 1945, when a number of agreements on arms control and disarmament were accompanied by additional steps to 'make credible' the provisions contained in these agreements. This also is taking place today:

---

6.   E. Schalger, *Conflict Resolution in the CSCE*, The Joan B. Kroc Institute for Peace Studies, University of Notre Dame, Indiana (Occasional Paper series 5: OP:4).

7.   In connection with the change in the name of this international body to Organization for Security and Co-operation in Europe (OSCE) at the summit in Budapest on 6 December 1994, following other publications the terms CSCE, OSCE (Organization for Security and Co-operation in Europe) or CSCE/OSCE will be used in this chapter depending on the period to which they refer.

8.   C. Marcinkowski and K. Paszkowski, *Dokument Wiedeński 1994*: Wprowadzenie [*Vienna Document 1994*: Introduction], Warsaw, 1995.

A number of arms control elements in force contain formal confidence-building measures (CBMs) that furnish codes of conduct for specific military situations (such as manoeuvres), call for the exchange of information designed to provide reassurance about peaceful intentions and suggest guidelines for the regulation of States' behaviour in crises.[9]

In the 1970s the first steps were taken in Europe to create an entire system of confidence-building measures, conceived to a certain degree as an autonomous structure 'aimed at neutralizing military force as an agent of change in international relations. The key attributes of such a system would be greater openness (less secrecy), predictability and stability.'[10]

Nearly twelve years later the Member States of the United Nations gave expression to their expectations concerning these measures. The conceptualization of confidence-building measures elaborated under the auspices of the Secretary-General is that the United Nations contains a holistic vision of these measures as procedures, instruments and mechanisms that can be used both on a worldwide and regional scale and even in a bilateral formula.[11] This vision still remains quite adequate for the reality of the present international order. At the same time, however, in some respects practice has outpaced the hypotheses, theses and recommendations put forward at the beginning of the 1980s.

Confidence-building measures are a worldwide phenomenon, albeit in a particular situation they can refer to multilateral relations on a worldwide, regional or even bilateral scale. None the less, it would be a mistake to assume that they can be applied to one selected geographical region. The fact is, however, that in some regions their development is more advanced than in others.

The nature and substantive scope of confidence-building measures is such that by their very essence they prevent differences of interests – between states and large social groups – from turning into conflicts whose outcome could be the threat of force. They can also be useful as instruments to prevent existing

---

9.   R. Berg, A. D. Rotfeld and A. Lynch (eds.), *Building Security in Europe*, New York, 1986, p. 13.

10. Ibid., p. 16.

11. Cf. Department of Political and Security Council Affairs, United Nations Centre for Disarmament, *Comprehensive Study on Confidence-building Measures* (Report of the Secretary-General), New York, United Nations, 1982.

The role of confidence-   89
building measures
in the prevention and
resolution of conflicts

differences of interests or their perception from escalating into crises and armed conflicts. This is preventive diplomacy as well, understood as 'action to prevent disputes from arising between parties, to prevent existing disputes from escalating into conflicts and to limit the spread of the latter when they occur'.[12]

An exceptionally important precondition for the success of anti-crisis actions on the borderline of confidence-building measures and preventive diplomacy turned out to be overcoming the international principle of consensus in effect in this structure. This was done by the Council of Ministers of the CSCE at a meeting in Prague when it accepted the principle – consensus minus one. This meant that in taking decisions in situations of the violation of the principles and agreements of the CSCE/OSCE, the state to blame for such violations can no longer block the decision of the organization bearing the marks of a political sanction against the agent of the violation.

DEVELOPMENT OF CONFIDENCE-BUILDING MEASURES IN EUROPE

In Europe, confidence-building measures since the middle of the 1970s have made a major contribution to easing East–West military confrontation and have then become the main instrument for reconstructing the foundations of the international security system, from confrontation to co-operation. Their development has encompassed three main areas: political, military and human rights.

The prevention of conflicts, controlling them and resolving disputes became the main area of activity of the OSCE after the cessation of East–West rivalry at the end of the 1980s. The direct cause of this fundamental reorientation of the activity of the OSCE was the lessening of international stability in the central-eastern part of the continent.[13] For at that time a number of new nations emerged

---

12. Boutros Boutros-Ghali, *An Agenda for Peace, Preventive Diplomacy, Peacemaking and Peacekeeping*, Report of the Secretary-General pursuant to the statement adopted by the Summit Meeting of the Security Council on 31 January 1992, para. 20, New York, United Nations, 1992.

13. For an assessment of the adaptation process of the CSCE/OSCE to the new conditions see J. M. Nowak, 'OBWE – między oczekiwaniami a rzeczywistościo (w XX-lecie istnienia)', *Sprawy Miêdzynarodowe* (Warsaw), No. 2, 1995, pp. 127–62.

from the great multinational structures and acted to regain/gain their own statehood. Two principles – the right of nations to self-determination and the right of states to territorial integrity – gave rise to numerous events with tragic consequences. This has been pointed out by analysts studying the causes of the bloody events in Eastern Europe and Central Asia.[14]

At the same time, the vast nationality, ethnic, cultural and linguistic mosaic of these areas, and their most often attendant general and economic backwardness, have repeatedly caused the drive for independence to erupt in the form of conflicts within states that threaten international stability. This situation endures to this day, and the prospects for a real improvement in the near future are not bright. This applies especially to multiethnic, multicultural and multilinguistic states, in particular to the former Yugoslavia and the former Soviet Union.

All this became the direct reason for intense actions on the part of CSCE/OSCE to build effective conflict-prevention, conflict-management and conflict-resolution instruments, procedures and mechanisms. It is to the credit of this organization that it reacted rather quickly to the fact that in the new geopolitical situation threats to peace and stability resulting from the threat of a sudden attack on a large scale by one state (or group of states) against other states have ceased to be the principal source of conflict. On the other hand, the main problem has become rampant nationalism, chauvinism, xenophobia, intolerance of national, ethnic and religious minorities.[15] The tragic events in the former Yugoslavia and the former Soviet Union testify all too eloquently to this. On the other hand, cases could be observed of the absolute insistence on their rights by some minorities. All this together caused the international situation in Europe to be less stable in the 1990s than during the period of bipolar East–West rivalry.

A change in the nature of the threats had to be attended by a suitable reconstruction of conflict-prevention, management and resolution measures, mechanisms and procedures. CSCE/OSCE succeeded in elaborating an entire set

---

14. Cf. G. Munuera, *Preventing Armed Conflict in Europe: Lessons from Recent Experience*, Paris, Institute for Security Studies, Western European Union, 1994 (Chaillot Papers, No. 15/16).

15. See, on this subject, A. D. Rotfeld, 'European Security Structures in Transition', *SIPRI Yearbook 1992*, pp. 563–83.

The role of confidence-
building measures
in the prevention and
resolution of conflicts   91

of such solutions. All of them are based on confidence-building measures in the broad sense. In the new conditions, early recognition of disputed questions and proper powers to act as well as the capacity to function in conditions in which disputed issues very often are traditionally reserved exclusively to the competence of states as their internal affairs began to be decisive. However, three spheres of issues continue to be the most important: political, military and human-rights questions.

In the wide range of anti-crisis instruments of the OSCE, confidence- and security-building measures occupy a prominent place. This is in keeping with the strategy of action adopted by this organization, a strategy that definitely favours counter-measures in the earliest possible phases of a crisis. In 1994, the Secretary-General of the OSCE, Dr W. Hoynek, stated on this subject:

In dealing with conflict situations at different stages of development, the activities of the CSCE range in principle from early warning to post-conflict measures. But the CSCE is giving clear emphasis to early warning and conflict prevention. This is the politically most opportune and, in terms of financing, cheapest approach.[16]

In accordance with this general approach, early warning should make it possible to take preventive measures as soon as possible. In this context, fact-finding activities are the top priority, because they make it possible to take the right decision as to the form, scope and time of further actions by the OSCE or its agenda. This concerns selecting the correct approach from the broad range of actions referred to by the common term 'preventive diplomacy'.

Today, the OSCE has at its disposal a wide range of possibilities of receiving early warning signals. These possibilities consist of a great diversity of frequent and systematic contacts and intense political consultations both within the structures and institutions of the OSCE itself and in structures connected in one way or another with this Organisation (EU, WEU, NATO, United Nations, Council of Europe).

The success of anti-crisis actions depends largely on how soon they are undertaken after receiving the early warning. The experience of the OSCE shows that 'the earlier the action is undertaken, the better the chances of peaceful

16.   W. Hoynek, 'Role of the CSCE and Other Organisations in Managing Crisis and Maintaining Peace', *Studia Diplomatica*, Vol. 47, No. 4, 1994, pp. 37–49.

solutions'.[17] The actions undertaken should take into consideration the magnitude and nature of the threat.

Early warning, the prevention of conflicts and resolution of crises is the major anti-crisis instrument of the OSCE. It is based on the following: (a) regular political consultations in the Permanent Council, Senior Council and Ministerial Council; (b) activities of the Chairman-in-Office (with his personal representatives); (c) the 'Troika'[18] and the Secretary-General; (d) political missions of the Supreme Commissioner for National Minorities, short missions (explanatory, reporting, experts); and (e) missions of the Office for Democratic Institutions and Human Rights. All these actions perform warning and prevention functions. Thus, they serve to settle disputes.[19]

The OSCE has elaborated three basic mechanisms for reacting to crisis situations – emergency mechanisms – depending on whether these crises are characterized by: (a) a serious and sudden worsening of the situation; (b) unusual military activity; and (c) serious violations of human rights. Each of these mechanisms entails a three-step procedure for explaining these situations: first, an attempt to explain in direct contact with the two sides engaged in the dispute (the party responsible for infringing the CSCE principles); second, consultations on the object of the dispute/accusation with the body of all members of the organization; and, third, an OSCE mission to verify the facts and to create political conditions for easing tensions and settling the dispute.

POLITICAL MEASURES

In speaking of confidence-building measures in political matters, we should note the fundamental nature of the ten principles contained in the 'Declaration on Principles Guiding Relations between Participating States', which is an essential part of the Helsinki Final Act. Being a development and adaptation to European

---

17.   Hoynek, op. cit.
18.   The 'Troika' consists of the present Secretatry-General of the OSCE, the past and the following one.
19.   For more on this subject, cf. P. Świtalski, 'Rola KBWE w rozwiązywaniu konfliktów', *Sprawy Międzynarodowe*, 1993, No. 4, pp. 27–50.

The role of confidence-
building measures
in the prevention and
resolution of conflicts   93

conditions of the principles adopted in the United Nations Charter, the Declaration of 1975 laid out a new direction for the development of international relations, and the observation of its norms even today is the foundation of the European order.[20]

The declarative wording of the 'philosophy' calls for a basic change in relations between states, namely, viewing one's own security not in the policy of maximum armaments and confrontation but in co-operation and self-limitation in the military sphere, and could become gradually manifested in substantively significant agreements on very practical questions. Among them were agreements on confidence-building measures.

In striving to increase the effectiveness of conflict prevention and resolution, the CSCE/OSCE states placed emphasis on strengthening the element of mutual political consultations and on increasing the capacity to identify the causes of conflicts. This also concerned tensions arising within states and threatening to erupt into international disputes.

As regards an early warning[21] that the situation threatens to erupt into a conflict, this role is performed by: (a) regular, deepened political consultations held within the aforementioned CSCE/OSCE structures; and (b) signals sent by the Senior Council, by each state directly involved in the dispute; a group of eleven states not directly involved in the dispute; the High Commissioner on National Minorities; the Consultative Committee of the Conflict Prevention Centre; the Human Dimension mechanism or the Valletta Principles for Dispute Settlement and Provisions for a Procedure for Peaceful Settlement of Disputes.

If a crisis arises, the Senior Council takes all the appropriate political measures to prevent the situation from becoming worse, recommending at the same time the use of good offices, mediation or conciliation. In connection with the situation, the Senior Council may also assign certain tasks to the Chairman-in-Office, to an ad hoc group and/or to the Consultative Committee of the Conflict Prevention Centre (CPC).

20. Final Act of the Conference on Security and Co-operation in Europe, Helsinki, 1 August 1975.
21. Cf. *Supplementary Document to Give Effect to Certain Provisions Contained in the Charter of Paris for a New Europe*, November 1990.

The following crisis-prevention and management instruments are employed:

- Fact-finding and rapporteur missions created on the basis of consensus by the Senior Council of the Consultative Committee of the CPC. Reports of the missions are submitted to the Senior Council of the Consultative Committee of the CPC. The costs are covered by all participating states.

- OSCE peace-keeping operations supplementing the political process of resolution of disputes.

- They can be undertaken 'in the event a dispute arises within or between states'.

- Peaceful settlement of disputes: Recognizing the obligation of states to settle disputes peacefully as the foundation of the CSCE process and as the basic components of the capacity of this institution to keep the peace and security in this part of the world, 'a comprehensive set of measures to expand the options available within the CSCE to assist states to resolve their disputes peacefully has been developed'. To this end, a comprehensive and coherent set of measures has been negotiated that contains the element of compulsion for conciliation procedures, a reconciliation-truce panel and other means.

In most cases, the involvement of the OSCE in anti-crisis actions starts with recommendations contained in reports from the personal missions of representatives of the Chairman-in-Office.

The role of the Chairman-in-Office and his personal representatives in employing techniques characteristic of confidence- and security-building measures in actions directed to prevent and settle conflicts is all-important. Practically speaking, this concerns all forms, manifestations and phases of action of the OSCE in these questions, especially the functioning of the early warning and early reaction system. Moreover, the scope of his practical powers in the context in question results from the fact that: (a) he shapes the composition, scope of authority and exercises supervision and assesses the work of the ad hoc groups formed in an emergency to provide additional assistance to the Chairman-in-Office, especially in the prevention of conflicts, management of crises and settlement of disputes; and (b) he determines and defines the mandate of personal representatives acting on his behalf 'in the event of a crisis or conflict'.[22]

The role of confidence-
building measures
in the prevention and
resolution of conflicts   95

The 'Berlin Mechanism'

In 1991 the CSCE created an 'emergency mechanism' for undertaking consultations and co-operation in cases of an urgent exceptional situation.[23] It boils down to the fact that in 'a serious emergency situation which may arise from a violation of one of the Principles of the Final Act or as the result of major disruptions endangering peace, security or stability', OSCE member states will without delay hold appropriate consultations and act jointly to remove such a threat. These consultations and joint action may also involve the following:

Every state – after reaching the conclusion that such a serious situation has arisen – may demand appropriate explanations from the country or countries directly involved in such a situation, within forty-eight hours.

If the situation remains unexplained, each of them may turn to the Chairman-in-Office of the Senior Council with a motion to convene an emergency meeting of the Council. All OSCE member states are immediately informed of this fact. The Chairman-in-Office also contacts the states involved in the matter within twenty-four hours.

If two or more states approve the motion and convene such a meeting, within forty-eight hours the Chairman-in-Office informs the member states of the date of such a meeting. However, it should take place no earlier than forty-eight hours and no later than three days after the notification.

This meeting – depending on the assessment of the situation – may accept recommendations or motions concerning the resolution of the problem. It may also suggest a meeting at ministerial level.[24]

22. These questions are regulated by the decisions reached at the Helsinki Summit II. Cf. 'Early Warning, Conflict Prevention and Crisis Management (including fact-finding and rapporteur missions and CSCE peacekeeping), Peaceful Settlement of Disputes', *Helsinki Summit Decisions*, Helsinki, 10 July 1992, part III. Ibid., paras. 3–22.
23. Document of the Berlin Meeting of the CSCE Council of Ministers, Berlin, 19–20 June 1991, Annex: 'Mechanism for Consultation and Co-operation with Regard to Emergency Situations', *Recueil de Documents*, No. 1, 1993, pp. 201–12.
24. Ibid., para. 2.13.

The 'Berlin Mechanism' as such is difficult to classify in 'classical' confidence-building measures. However, it is a mechanism for whose functioning these measures are the starting point.

MILITARY AND SECURITY-RELATED MEASURES

As emphasized earlier, confidence-building measures by their nature may be treated as instruments for preventing armed conflicts. This is true in particular of measures in effect in the sphere of military matters. However, they cannot be treated as instruments for resolving such conflicts. Their action as an anti-crisis instrument is in a certain sense preventive, deeply precautionary. The functioning of a whole range of structures, mechanisms and procedures constituting the essence of confidence-building measures makes it possible to activate mechanisms and procedures for resolving disputes between states.

The military confidence-building measures in effect today concern the following crucial questions:[25]

Information about armed forces and armaments as well as plans in this area.

Reducing the risk of an alarming situation from arising.

Contacts between military establishments.

Prior notifications about particular kinds of military activities.

Observation of particular kinds of military activity.

Changes in annual plans of military activity.

The system for supervision over agreed upon undertakings.

Establishment of a system of direct communication.

In particular, the following obligations in effect in this area are of fundamental importance for the prevention of conflicts:

Annual exchanges of military information reflecting the state of their armed forces; the main systems of armament and ordnance; plans for distributing main systems of armament and ordnance; notification of their defence plans;

---

25.   Vienna Document 1994, para. 9–159, Vienna, 28 November 1994.

The role of confidence-   97
building measures
in the prevention and
resolution of conflicts

making available additional explanatory information connected with the contents of the information provided.[26]

Consultations and co-operation to explain 'all unusual and unplanned activities of their armed forces' of a 'significant nature'; co-operation in particular concerning 'dangerous incidents of a military nature' and 'voluntary acceptance of visits for the purpose of allaying fears connected with military activity'.[27]

Organization of visits to their air bases for representatives of other states 'for the purpose of giving the visitors the possibility of observing the activities of the air base'; promoting and facilitating the exchange of military contacts and military co-operation; organizing shows of new types of armaments and ordnance.[28]

Prior notification (forty-two days) of the commencement, defined in a special way in the basic document, of military activity.[29]

Inviting representatives of other states to observe military exercises.[30]

Exchange of annual calendar plans of their military activities planned for the following year.[31]

---

26. Ibid., paras. 9–15.9.
27. Ibid., paras. 16–18.2.
28. Ibid., paras. 19–35.
29. Ibid., paras. 36–44. This concerns military activity with the participation of at least 9,000 soldiers or at least 250 combat tanks or at least 50 armoured combat vehicles or at least 250 self-propelled and pulled artillery pieces, mortars, multiple-address rocket launchers (calibre 100 mm), or if the forces participating in such activity 'shall be organized in the complement of a division or at least two brigades/regiment, not necessarily subordinated to the same division'.
30. Ibid., para. 45–58. This concerns exercises with the participation of at least 13,000 soldiers or 300 combat tanks or 500 armoured combat vehicles or 500 self-propelled and pulled artillery pieces, mortars and multi-address rocket launchers. As regards amphibious, helicopter or parachute landing operations, the admissible limit here is 3,500 soldiers.
31. Ibid., paras. 59–64.

Scrupulous observance of provisions limiting the magnitude and intensity of military activity.[32]

Respect for the right of every state to conduct inspections on the territory of other states and to permit all other states to make inspections on its territory (at least three times a year). Inspection from the ground, air or both of these ways is permitted.[33]

Participation in the functioning of a direct communication system between the capitals of all states for the rapid transmission of information connected with the activity of the confidence- and security-building measures system. Contact points operating round the clock are connected with this.[34]

Participation every year of the representatives of all states to assess the function of the system as such.[35]

These measures are actions that regulate and in principle limit the military activity of the signatory states. Despite the fact that they do not have an important influence on the structure and size of the military potential at the disposal of states, they nevertheless seriously limit the possibility of an armed attack by one state on another, especially a large-scale sudden attack. The observance of the obligations entered into is the object of multi-aspect control of a special

---

32.   Vienna Document, paras. 65–69. States may conduct: (a) only one military activity subject to prior notification in the course of two years with the participation of more than 40,000 soldiers or 900 combat tanks; (b) not more than six operations in the course of a calendar year with the participation of more than 13,000 soldiers or 300 combat tanks but not more than 40,000 soldiers or 900 combat tanks; (c) among these six operations states in the course of one calendar year may conduct only three operations with the participation of more than 25,000 soldiers or 400 combat tanks; (d) states may not conduct more than three military operations simultaneously with the participation in each of more than 13,000 soldiers or 300 combat tanks; (e) by 15 November of every year each state shall send information to all other OSCE member states concerning a military operation with the participation of more than 40,000 soldiers or 900 combat tanks. Failure to send such information means lack of consent to such activity.

33.   Ibid., paras. 70–104.

34.   Ibid., paras. 130–144.

35.   Ibid., paras. 145–153. Annual implementation assessment meetings take place at the forum of the Conflict Prevention Centre.

The role of confidence-
building measures
in the prevention and
resolution of conflicts   99

international body. This body has formal, institutional and material-technical possibilities to determine and signal all irregularities in the performance of the provisions by states. Thus they give these instruments the nature of conflict-prevention measures.[36]

'Code of Conduct . . . '

The second basic document establishing the politico-military criteria of conduct of the OSCE states is the 'Code of Conduct on Politico-Military Aspects of Security'.[37]

The Budapest Summit established the politico-military standards of conduct of the OSCE states.[38] The degree of observance by individual members of the community of the standards of the Code indirectly shows the degree to which they observe the rules accepted by the community as a whole. It also indirectly signals the state of security on the entire continent.

These agreements are close in nature to 'classical' confidence-building measures. Despite the fact that formally they are not part of the aforementioned system, on account of their nature the measures contained in the 'Code of Conduct on Politico-Military Aspects of Security' supplement and strengthen it in an important way by preventing situations from arising in which tensions of various kinds within and between countries could result in the use of force.

This document, unequivocally based on the principle of the non-use of force in the resolution of all disputes, emphasizes the prevention and resolution of disputes by peaceful means. It formulates the following principles of conduct:

Every violation of the norms established by the OSCE obligates states to hold consultations without delay with the state awaiting assistance in realization of the right to individual or collective self-defence.

36. Periodic analyses of assessments of the functioning of this system by Z. Lachowski are published successively by the Stockholm International Peace Research Institute in the yearbook, *World Armaments and Disarmament*.

37. 'Code of Conduct on Politico-Military Aspects of Security' is part IV of the Budapest Document 1994. *Towards a Genuine Partnership in a New Era*, Budapest, 6 December 1994, paras. 5–57. Polish edition: Warsaw, PISM, 1995, pp. 31–8.

38. The draft of such a document was submitted by Poland on 11 November 1992 at the CSCE Forum for Co-operation on Security.

It obligates all states to act in solidarity to combat terrorism in all its forms and, in connection therewith, to fulfil the requirements of international agreements by which they are bound to prosecute and extradite terrorists.

It obligates all states not to provide assistance to or support states that are in violation of their obligation to refrain from the threat or use of force against the territorial or political independence of any state, or in any other manner inconsistent with the Charter of the United Nations and with the Declaration on Principles Guiding Relations between Participating States contained in the Helsinki Final Act.

It confirms the inalienable right of each state to individual and collective self-defence and to choose freely its own security arrangements, and also confirms the sovereign right of each state to belong to any organization, to enter into alliances or to remain neutral.

Each participating state will maintain 'only such military capabilities as are commensurate with individual or collective legitimate security needs'. No participating state will attempt to impose military domination over any other participating state, and will determine its military capabilities on the basis of national democratic procedures, bearing in mind the legitimate security concerns of other states:

It obligates participating states to implement in good faith all commitments in the field of arms control, disarmament and confidence- and security-building and to develop other efforts in this area.

It obligates the participating states to counter tensions that may lead to conflict. The sources of such tensions include violations of human rights, nationalism, racism, chauvinism, xenophobia and anti-Semitism. It stresses the importance of early identification of potential conflicts, their prevention, control and peaceful settlement. In the event of armed conflict, they will seek to facilitate the effective cessation of hostilities and seek to create conditions favourable to a political solution of the conflict.

It postulates that participating states will consider the democratic political control of military, paramilitary and internal security forces as well as of intelligence services and the police to be an indispensable element of stability and security. Moreover, participating states will further the integration of their armed forces with civil society as an important expression of democracy. They will also provide for guidance to, and control of, their military by constitutionally established authorities. On the other hand, the armed forces will remain politically neutral, and paramilitary forces will refrain from the acquisition of combat mission capabilities in excess of those for which they were established. The recruitment or call-up of personnel for service in the military or paramilitary forces will be consistent with respect for human rights and fundamental freedoms.

Each participating state will ensure that its armed forces are commanded, trained and equipped in ways that are consistent with the provisions of international law. Its military and defence policy will also be consistent with international law, and any decision to assign its armed forces to missions will be in conformity with constitutional procedures. Participating states also will not use armed forces to limit the peaceful and lawful exercise of their human and civil rights by persons as individuals or as representatives of groups nor to deprive them of their national, religious, cultural, linguistic or ethnic identity.

Each participating state is responsible for implementation of the Code, and may be asked to provide additional clarification regarding its implementation.[39]

Two other agreements also play an essential role in the European anti-crisis system and are an integral part of the continental system: the Treaty on Conventional Armed Forces in Europe[40] and the enlarged control and inspection system it contains, which is based on: (a) exchange of periodic information on the size of conventional land and air forces and all changes in their size, distribution, the kinds of types of armament, command structure, organization, etc.; and (b) on-the-spot control, inspections from the air and data gathering by technical means (satellite data). In addition, the signatories are obligated, on the principle of reciprocity, to provide each other with a total of thirteen kinds of basic

---

39. See note 37 above.
40. 'Treaty on Conventional Forces in Europe', Paris, 19 November 1990, *Recueil de Documents*, 1992, No. 4, pp. 126–66.

information. A special body, the Joint Consultative Group, oversees the observance by the parties to the treaty of its basic provisions.[41]

The control and inspection mechanism, together with a parallel system of confidence-building measures, creates the core of a comprehensive and effective set of agreements for constant observation of current changes and trends in the size and profile of the military potential of states in Europe; it also enables accurate forecasts of eventual important changes in this area. This affords great possibilities for an accurate identification of the intentions of states in their security policy, and this means conflict prevention.

The second agreement is the Treaty on Open Skies,[42] containing the consent of the signatories to reconnaissance flights over their territories by the other states parties to the treaty for the purpose of gathering information about the military potential on these territories. The territorial scope of the treaty extends over an area from Vladivostok to Vancouver and covers the entire territories of the states. Other states not belonging to the OSCE may also accede to the treaty.

The second emergency mechanism, the Vienna Mechanism, is conceptually similar to confidence-building measures. It is based on the provisions of Part II of the Vienna Document 1994 entitled: 'Mechanism for Consultation and Co-operation in Unusual Military Activity'.[43] Pursuant to the provisions contained in this chapter, states are obligated to undertake consultations and co-operation in the event of the 'unusual and unplanned activities of their armed forces . . . which are of a significant nature . . . as to which other participating states express concern for their security'.[44] Apprehensive states may call upon the state where such activity is taking place for an explanation. The latter should give an answer within 48 hours. All OSCE states will be informed without delay about this question and the answer. If the answer does not satisfy the inquiring state, it can propose a meeting to the answering state within forty-eight hours. This proposal is submitted to all other OSCE states. The state giving the answer may invite other interested states to the meeting. The state requesting the meeting may propose a

---

41.   Cf. 'Protocol on the Joint Consultative Group'.
42.   'Treaty on Open Skies', 24 March 1992, Helsinki.
43.   Ibid., paras. 16–18.2.
44.   Ibid., para. 16.

The role of confidence-
building measures
in the prevention and
resolution of conflicts

103

meeting of all participating states within forty-eight hours. The presence at such a meeting is mandatory for all states involved in the matter. Depending on the assessment of a given situation, the Permanent Council shall take appropriate measures to settle it. All of this does not preclude the possibility of voluntary visits to the state on whose territory the disturbing military activities are taking place.[45] Confidence-building measures in military matters perform per se an exceptionally important stabilizing and anti-crisis role in international relations in every corner of the globe. This results from the role that military force continues to play both in international relations and within individual countries. This general thesis relates first and foremost to Europe, where after the fundamental systemic changes of the late 1980s, the greatest depreciation of the role of military force took place and where the threat of a 'big war' now belongs to the past. For these means to be more effective, they ought to be applied to present European realities, in particular to the change in the threats. The latter now have their sources less in relations between states and more in the conflict-creating events within states.

CONFIDENCE-BUILDING MEASURES
IN HUMANITARIAN FIELDS

Today, threats to peace and international stability more often originate in cases of a serious violation of basic human rights. So it is not surprising that the protection of human rights is now at the centre of attention.

This began modestly in 1975 with the acceptance in Helsinki of postulates for a gradual elimination of barriers in contacts between citizens of the East and West, facilitation in the exchange of information between countries, and the expansion of co-operation between them in culture, science and education.[46] In time, with the normalization of international relations, the field of humanitarian affairs, constituting an integral part of the Helsinki process, expanded and in 1990, after the revolutionary changes in Central Europe, became the basic element of

45. Ibid., para. 18.
46. 'Co-operation in Humanitarian and Other Fields' of the Final Act of the Conference on Security and Co-operation in Europe, Helsinski, 1 August 1975.

this process – an element on which the future European order was to be based. In 1990 the CSCE states asserted that 'full respect for human rights and fundamental freedoms and the development of societies based on pluralistic democracy and the rule of law are prerequisites for progress in setting up the lasting order of peace, security, justice and co-operation that they seek to establish in Europe'.[47] The CSCE Summit in Paris, in the historic document 'Charter of Paris for a New Europe' of November 1990, made respect for human rights, democracy and the rule of law the cornerstone of the post-Yalta European order, thereby confirming the traditional attachment of the CSCE for the human dimension.[48]

Bearing in mind the elimination of the causes of international disputes and conflicts resulting from the violation of human rights, the CSCE states, especially during the period of transformation, directed their attention to

ensure full respect for human rights and fundamental freedoms, to abide by the rule of law, to promote the principles of democracy and, in this regard, to build, strengthen and protect democratic institutions, as well as to promote tolerance throughout society.[49]

In this context, the Helsinki II Summit strengthened the system for controlling compliance with CSCE obligations and the development of co-operation in the human dimension. The Office for Democratic Institutions and Human Rights[50] created on the recommendation of the Paris Summit as the main institution in the human dimension was given a mandate to control the implementation of actions by states in this field. These actions would 'contribute to early warning in the prevention of conflicts'.[51]

---

47. 'Document of the Copenhagen Meeting of the Conference on the Human Dimension of the CSCE', Copenhagen, 29 June 1990, *Recueil de Documents*, No. 2, pp. 105 et seq.
48. One of the practical manifestations of this attachment was acceptance of the principles of free elections to representative bodies and the establishment of a new CSCE institution, i.e. Office for Free Elections, with its seat in Warsaw.
49. 'Human Dimension', Art. 2 of the Helsinki II Document.
50. The CSCE Summit in Paris established the institution of High Commissioner for Elections, which after a short time was transformed into the High Commissioner on National Minorities (HCNM).
51. Ibid., para. 6.

The role of confidence-
building measures
in the prevention and
resolution of conflicts   105

The mechanisms and procedures created by CSCE/OSCE in recent years to deal with serious violations of human rights are a rather effective anti-crisis instrument, in particular early informing of international opinion about cases of tensions and threats for international stability arising in this context.[52] Such tensions can be rather effectively neutralized by the use of these instruments. The preventive nature of these procedures and mechanisms has much in common, as regards methods of action, with typical confidence-building measures.

The Moscow Mechanism

The Conference on the Human Dimension of the CSCE in Moscow (4 October 1991) made an important modification of existing provisions in the human dimension that had been established earlier in Vienna and later in Copenhagen. The changes introduced at the Moscow meeting reduced the waiting time for reaction by the state to which written notification was addressed concerning the violation of basic human rights. The deadline was shortened to ten days (paragraph 2). In turn a two-side explanatory meeting should take place no later than one week from the date of lodging the appropriate motion.

The Human Dimension Mechanism, which has not been used very often so far, nevertheless has turned out to be an effective instrument for the prevention and moderation of conflicts.

As in the Berlin Mechanism, problems in the field of human rights causing tensions may be, in the second instance, investigated by experts, a list of whom is in the OSCE. From this group the interested state[53] can create a mission composed of a maximum of three persons which will attempt to resolve the problem in the observation of human rights. Without delay this state will inform the OSCE, which

---

52. In particular, this refers to decisions taken in this field by: (a) Vienna Final Document 1989; (b) Document of the Copenhagen Meeting of the Conference on the Human Dimensions of the CSCE, Copenhagen, 29 June 1990; (c) Document of the Moscow Meeting of the Conference of the Human Dimension of the CSCE, Moscow, 3 October 1991; (d) Vienna Declaration adopted at the Council of Europe Summit, Vienna, 9 October 1993; (e) Decisions by the CSCE Council of Ministers: CSCE and the New Europe – Our Security is Indivisible, Rome, November/December 1993, para. 5.
53. Moscow Document, para. 4.

will give this mission all possible support, and send information about the creation of the team to all other member states.

The task of the mission of experts 'is to facilitate resolution of a particular question or problem relating to the human dimension of the CSCE'. Such a mission may gather the information necessary for carrying out tasks and, as appropriate, use its good offices and mediation services to promote dialogue and co-operation among interested parties.[54] The inviting state in addition may implement other actions such as 'fact-finding and advisory services in order to suggest ways and means of facilitating the observance of CSCE commitments'. In turn, Article 12 of the Moscow Document stipulates that each participating state, after reaching the conclusion that

a particularly serious threat to the fulfilment of the provisions of the CSCE human dimension has arisen in another participating state, it may with the support of at least nine other participating states engage the procedure set forth in para. 10. On the other hand based on the provisions contained in para. 11, any participating state may request that the Senior Council create a mission of CSCE experts of rapporteurs.

The anti-crisis instrument of the CSCE/OSCE in the human dimension was strengthened significantly in 1993 by the provision that 'the decision-making bodies of the CSCE will consider human-dimension issues on a regular basis as an internal part of deliberations relating to European security'.[55]

The High Commissioner on National Minorities (HCNM)

The sharp animosities and armed conflicts on an ethnic basis that erupted at the beginning of the 1990s in a number of Eastern European countries became the direct impulse for the establishment in 1992 of the High Commissioner on National Minorities,[56] whose task is to study minorities problems that are a potential threat to European security.

---

54.   Moscow Document, para. 5.
55.   Documents of the CSCE Council of Ministers Meeting, Rome, 1 December 1993.
56.   For more on the origins of this institution and its powers see: A. Bloed (ed.), *The Conference on Security and Co-operation in Europe. Analysis and Basic Documents 1972–1993*, London/Boston/Dordrecht, 1993; M. Jeziorski, 'Wysoki Komisarz do Spraw Mniejszości Narodowych [The CSCE High Commissioner on National Minorities]', *Sprawy Międzynarodowe*, No. 2, 1992, PUSM, pp. 135–52.

The role of confidence-
building measures
in the prevention and
resolution of conflicts   107

The founders of this institution were aware that the protection of persons belonging to national minorities goes beyond the framework of the human dimension of the CSCE. On the other hand, it is clearly stressed that

[the] mandate does not obligate the High Commissioner to act on behalf of the observation by participating states of the obligations contained in CSCE documents in respect to human rights, including persons belonging to national minorities. The High Commissioner – as the mandate clearly emphasizes – concentrates on preventing conflicts.[57]

This was a unique institution that had no counterpart in any other international organization at the time. Thanks to the fact that it has been given certain powers, it has the opportunity of becoming 'the most elaborated and most intrusive CSCE instrument of conflict prevention'.[58]

The intention of the founders was for this institution to become 'an instrument for the prevention of conflicts in the earliest possible stage'. The task of the HCNM is to provide early warning and, if called for, early reaction on the part of the OSCE. Thus the aim is to provide this organization with reliable information about tensions that have the potential of erupting into conflicts between states.

Although the High Commissioner acts under the aegis of the Senior Council, he has considerable independence from the decisions of the OSCE political structures.[59] He has a great degree of freedom in choosing the sources of information about the situation of national minorities in a given country.[60] At the earliest stage of a tense situation it is up to him to assess its nature, the role of the parties involved and its possible implications. If he reaches the conclusion that his consultations are ineffective and that there is a risk of a conflict, he may send an early warning. His addressee is the Senior Council, which will investigate the

---

57. Jeziorski, op. cit., p. 142.
58. A. Bloed, 'The CSCE Conflict Prevention Mechanisms and Procedures', *CSCE Office for Democratic Institutions and Human Rights Bulletin*, Vol. 2, No. 3, 1994, pp. 30–3.
59. This is confirmed by the Chairman-in-Office himself. Cf. Max van der Stoel, 'The Role of the CSCE High Commissioner on National Minorities', *Studia Diplomatica*, Vol. 25, No. 4, 1994, pp. 59–70.
60. Ibid.

matter in accordance with a set procedure. Such a warning may activate the Mechanism of Urgent Consultations – a special procedure foreseen for such situations. The High Commissioner, with the consent of the Senior Council, may make further contacts with the parties involved in the dispute 'for the purpose of searching for possible solutions'. He may also draw on the help of experts, who act in a given matter within the mandate accorded to him. This is a form of early reaction on the part of the Senior Council, which gives him far-reaching powers for more advanced actions in order to reach settlements to diminish the tension.[61]

The powers of the HCNM have been defined rather modestly, for they only include 'the promotion of dialogue and confidence-building by bringing parties together at the negotiation table and by mediating between the parties'.

The opinion has been expressed that his mandate is not very specific and may make it difficult for him to act effectively. These imprecise formulae are the result of the compromise reached in 1992 among all CSCE states. One positive aspect of this vagueness is the possibility of acting flexibly. The main mission of the HCNM is to bring about a de-escalation of tensions by supporting dialogue, confidence and co-operation between the parties involved in the dispute. His main instrument is to send formal information (notice) of early warning, hence this is more of a theoretical power. It has been argued that over-zealousness on the part of the High Commissioner in sending such a signal might indicate the failure of his mission as a person attempting to reduce and remove the sources of tension. Hence such an overreaction is not conducive to his mission, because

the involved parties would want, as much as possible, to maintain control of the situation, and an issuance of early warning would bring the problem to the table of political CSCE bodies . . . there is a potential dilemma that an involvement by the High Commissioner may lead to an actual escalation of a conflict.[62]

As a consequence of such conduct, the adversaries might be less willing to compromise.

---

61. For these reasons this is rightly regarded as 'the most elaborated and most intrusive OSCE instrument of conflict prevention'.
62. A. Bloed, 'The CSCE and Protection of National Minorities', *CSCE Bulletin*, Vol. 1, No. 3, 1993, p. 1.

The role of confidence- 109
building measures
in the prevention and
resolution of conflicts

The second question raised on various occasions is co-ordination of the actions of the High Commissioner with other structures acting in the field of human rights.

In the four years of the activities of this institution, nearly all the sources of ethnic tensions in Eastern Europe have been on the list of the 'quiet diplomacy' and fact-finding missions of the HCNM and his experts: Estonia, Latvia, Slovakia, Hungary, Romania, former Yugoslavia, the Former Yugoslav Republic of Macedonia, Albania, Kazakhstan, Kyrgyzstan and the ever-present problem of the Sinti and Roma.[63]

Despite the fact that the recommendations of the HCNM are not binding on the parties, on account of the fact that he enjoys the political support of the CSCE his recommendations are carefully taken into consideration.[64]

The Office for Democratic Institutions and Human Rights (ODIHR)

In the system for controlling compliance with the obligations of the CSCE/OSCE and the development of co-operation in the field of the human dimension, an extremely important role is played by the Office for Democratic Institutions and Human Rights in Warsaw (ODIHR).[65] The main goal of this structure 'is to assist the participating states of the OSCE to build democratic institutions and implement their human dimension commitments'.[66]

The main tasks of the ODIHR functioning under the general supervision of the Committee of High Representatives consist in giving assistance in:

---

63. The reports of these missions were published in the *OSCE Bulletin*.
64. For more details on this institution and the activities of the High Commissioner, see M. Jeziorski, 'Wysoki Komisarz KBWE do spraw Mniejszości Narodowych', *Sprawy Międzynarodowe* (Warsaw), No. 2, 1994, pp. 135–52.
65. The predecessor of the ODIHR was the Office for Free Elections in Warsaw created by a decision taken at the CSCE Summit in Paris. Its task was 'to facilitate contacts and exchange of information on elections within participating states'. The more specific scope of activities of this structure was due to the provisions adopted in the 1990s by the Copenhagen Meeting of the Conference on the Human Dimension of the CSCE (paras. 6, 7 and 8).
66. *OSCE Office for Democratic Institutions and Human Rights Bulletin*, Vol. 4, No. 4, 1996, pp. 29–30.

Controlling the carrying out of the commitments of states in this field (*inter alia* serving as a place of periodic multilateral meetings to discuss problems connected with observation of the human dimension in the member states; elaborating and submitting for discussion reports on the human dimension).

Playing the role of a centre for the exchange of information in this field (on aid programmes, the functioning of democratic institutions on the local/regional level).

Supporting other related actions (organizing seminars on the democratic process, especially in newly admitted states).

Taking early-warning and conflict-prevention actions.

The current priorities in the activities of the ODIHR are as follows:

Supporting the Programme for the Recovery and Development of Bosnia and Herzegovina.

Co-ordinating election monitoring processes.

Integrating human dimension issues into the work of the Permanent Council and monitoring the implementation of human dimension commitments.

Working with the Chairman-in-Office, particularly by providing early warning reports.

Providing co-ordinated legal support.

Assisting in the process of the building of civil societies, working with NGOs, national democratic institutions and with the media.

Providing information about the human dimension.

Working as a contact point for Roma and Sinti issues.

Working on migration issues.

Providing support to the OSCE missions with respect to their human dimension activities.[67]

---

67.   *OSCE Office for Democratic Institutions and Human Rights Bulletin*, Vol. 4, No. 4, 1996, pp. 29-30.

The role of confidence-
building measures
in the prevention and
resolution of conflicts

111

CONCLUSIONS

The conception of confidence-building measures strikes at the heart of the matter in respect to elimination of the causes of disputes and, if disputes do arise, to prevent them from escalating into crises and armed conflicts. The essence of these measures is identification at the earliest possible stage of tensions that could become the reason for a dispute. Widest possible knowledge on the sources of tensions should determine the nature of the preventive measures. Every action that contributes to easing tensions between antagonistic sides may be a confidence-building measure. So it is not surprising that in principle every unilateral action that is viewed positively by the opposite side is a confidence-building measure. Likewise, every bilateral or multilateral settlement of any question which until then caused anxiety in mutual relations is a confidence-building measure.

Some 'classical' confidence-building measures, especially those pertaining to military matters, should be modernized to work more effectively as tension- and conflict-prevention measures. To a greater degree than heretofore, confidence-building measures should be extended to internal and paramilitary forces.

The functioning of all kinds of confidence-building measures requires greater political attention, greater financial resources and highly qualified personnel.

Peace agreements as instruments for the resolution of intrastate conflicts

Emmanuel Roucounas

One of the main features of the post-Second World War era has been the growing number of internal conflicts and civil wars. The end of the Cold War has had an impact on the termination of some of these conflicts although other new instances have arisen. Mainly in the last fifty years, international law has encompassed in its rules situations not meeting the traditional definition of war between states, in order to bring under its aegis – thus containing their actions – all the actors of these armed conflicts, the government in place, revolutionary movements, insurgents, rebel groups and individuals.[1] At the same time armed internal conflicts lead to the conclusion of certain agreements or accords between the conflicting parties which endeavour to prevent repetition of hostilities by adopting specific measures for the restoration of peace and the creation of solid domestic institutions to that end.

The present study purports to examine how this transition from armed conflict to peace may be achieved by such agreements which, although of a defective legal nature, are nevertheless governed by elementary rules of

---

1.   O. Schachter, 'Internal Conflicts and International Law', R. S. Pathak and R. P. Dhokalia (eds.), in *International Law in Transition. Essays in Memory of Judge N. Singh*, pp. 1 et seq., Dordrecht/Boston/London, Kluwer AC, 1992; G.Abi-Saab, 'Non-international Armed Conflicts', *International Dimensions of Humanitarian Law*, pp. 217 et seq., Geneva/Paris, Henry-Dunant Institute/UNESCO, Kluwer AC, 1988; A. Eide, 'Internal Disturbances and Tensions', ibid., pp. 241 et seq.; K.-J. Partsch, 'Humanität im Bürgerkrieg', *Festschrift für H. J. Schlochauer*, 1981, pp. 515 et seq.

international law and signal the way towards the establishment of a democratic society based on the rule of law. The problems encountered are complex and, in the attempt to distinguish some common characteristics of such peace accords, we should always bear in mind that each case has its unique aspects and generalization beyond a certain limit may often be partly deceptive.

WHO IS SUBMITTED TO HUMANITARIAN RULES AND WHO RESPONDS FOR THEIR VIOLATION?

The tendency to submit internal conflicts to some legal guarantees began with the introduction of specific, though skeleton, provisions in the international instruments on humanitarian law. Hence common Article 3 of the four Geneva Conventions of 1949 which addresses situations of civil war and constitutes a miniature treaty[2] in favour of the protected persons. In a step forward, during the Geneva Diplomatic Conference on Humanitarian Law (1974–77), national liberation movements were separated from other revolutionary movements and have since been upgraded and submitted to the rules of Additional Protocol I (1977) which regulates conflicts of an international character.[3] For armed conflicts that are not of an international character Additional Protocol II (1977) further amplifies common Article 3 of the 1949 Geneva Conventions. The violation of these rules engages the criminal responsibility of the authors (whether acting on behalf of the state or not) under international law. According to the traditional but rather outdated theory of the 'subjects of international law',[4] this situation is perfectly explained by the fact that individuals are destinees of rights and obligations through an international treaty (the Geneva Conventions and Protocols) or custom. Today we witness the forceful applicability of general international law, not only in interstate relations and in the functioning of

---

2.   J. Pictet, *Commentary of the 1949 Geneva Convention IV*, pp. 35 et seq., Geneva, International Committee of the Red Cross, 1958.

3.   G.Abi-Saab, 'Wars of National Liberation in the Geneva Conventions and Protocols', *Recueil des Cours de l'Académie de droit international de La Haye*, Vol. 4, 1979, pp. 353 et seq.

4.   See R. Higgins, 'International Law and the Avoidance, Containment and Resolution of Disputes', *Recueil des Cours de l'Académie de droit international de La Haye*, Vol. 5, 1991, pp. 79–87.

Peace agreements as
instruments for
the resolution of
intrastate conflicts

115

international organizations but also as a supporting framework for the creation of rights and duties for individuals without necessarily entering into the question of the subjects of international law. The expansion of the international law of human rights testifies this evolution.

PARTIES IN CIVIL WAR

Historically, international law was marked by a two-tiered evolution in the effort to regulate situations arising from insurgency and expanding into belligerency. Insurgency has been defined as 'a half-way house between essentially ephemeral, spasmodic or unrecognized civil disorders, and the conduct of unrecognized war between contending factions within a state';[5] on the other hand, belligerency is taken as a status recognized either by foreign states or the government in place in cases where the insurgents occupy and administer a substantial portion of national territory and conduct hostilities through organized armed forces.[6] The dichotomy between insurgency and belligerency helped third states to organize relations with both parties to the conflict and to procure the protection of their citizens within the territory of a state in civil war.

As for the behaviour of the parties in the conduct of hostilities, the international instruments do not address the question of the legal quality of the parties. Article 1, paragraph 1, of the Additional Protocol II entitled 'Material Field of Application' speaks of the conflict that 'is taking place in the territory of a High Contracting Party between its armed forces' and 'dissident armed forces or other organized armed groups which, under responsible command, exercise such control at a part of the territory as to enable them to carry out sustained and concerted military operations and to implement [the] Protocol'. The question of the sovereignty of the state is not supposed to be affected (Article 3, para. 1),[7] and

---

5.   Lord A. McNair and Sir A. Watts, *The Legal Effects of War*, p. 30, Cambridge, 1966.
6.   Ibid., pp. 32–4.
7.   See, however, R. Provost, 'Problems of Indeterminacy and Characterization in the Application of Humanitarian Law', in M. Sellers (ed.), *The New World Order: Sovereignty, Human Rights and the Self-Determination of Peoples*, pp. 177 et seq., Oxford/New York, Berg Publishers, 1996.

the text refers to the 'state party' on the one hand and the 'adverse party' with no other qualifications. It states explicitly that 'nothing in the Protocol shall be invoked for the purpose of affecting the sovereignty of a state or the responsibility of the government, by all legitimate means, to maintain or re-establish law and order'. What international law prohibits by the aforesaid instruments and by customary international law are abuses and flagrant violations of human rights during armed conflicts occurring within the boundaries of a single state and not necessarily involving foreign participation.

PEACE AGREEMENTS: NATURE AND GOVERNING LAW

At some point, intrastate armed conflict comes to an end. If one of the parties is completely defeated, there is no agreement at all. But in most cases the cessation of hostilities is the result of a long and difficult process of third-party mediation and the realization by the parties to the armed conflict that they cannot change the course of the situation; the population is exhausted and the international community is ready to take or toughen measures against them. The conditions of termination of the civil war are inscribed in a written text, generally qualified as a 'peace agreement' or 'peace accord', 'framework agreement', 'settlement plan', 'basic agreement', etc. (hereinafter 'peace agreement'). The international community is never absent from the negotiation, formulation, signature and implementation of such an important instrument. All the peace agreements we shall now examine were concluded through outside instigation, encouragement and even pressure.[8] This means first and foremost a sustained action by the United Nations,[9] by regional organizations[10] and by states directly interested in

---

8.   R. Goy, 'Quelques accords récents mettant fin à des guerres civiles', *Annuaire français de droit international*, 1992, pp. 112 et seq.

9.   G. L. Burci, 'United Nations Peacekeeping Operations in Situations of Internal Conflict' in Sellers, op. cit., note 7, pp. 237–72, distinguishes five main categories of United Nations action in peace-keeping: monitoring and supervisory functions; humanitarian assistance to and protection of populations; disarmament of armed factions; institution-building; and organization of elections and referenda. See also Y. Daudet (ed.), *Les Nations Unies et la restauration de l'État*, Paris, Pédone, Rencontres Internationales de l'Institut d'Études Politiques d'Aix-en-Provence, 1995.

Peace agreements as
instruments for
the resolution of
intrastate conflicts 117

the cessation of hostilities.[11] It has nowadays become clear that the threshold of transition from domestic to international conflict is not situated in the crossing or otherwise of the frontiers between states or in the involvement of two or more states in the armed conflict. The threshold is one of magnitude. An armed conflict of a certain degree of importance is a threat to international peace and security whoever its actors are, and in that sense it leads to the mobilization of and action by the competent organs of the United Nations.

The problem of the legal nature of an instrument such as a peace agreement is not an easy one. As we know, the main characteristic of a treaty is that it is an agreement concluded between states or between states and international organizations, or between international organizations, and governed by international law.[12] With the exception of the 1991 Paris Agreements on Cambodia[13] and the 1995 Dayton/Paris General Framework Agreement on Bosnia and Herzegovina,[14] which are international treaties,[15] we cannot pretend

10. Burci, op.cit., pp. 237–8, stresses the fact that the sharp increase during recent years of peace-keeping operations by the United Nations is explained by the failure of regional organizations to cope with conflict situations in the post-Cold War era.

11. See, however, Y. Akashi, 'The Limits of UN Diplomacy and the Future of Conflict Mediation', *Survival*, 1995/96, pp. 83–98.

12. Article 1 of the 1969 Vienna Convention on the Law of Treaties; article of the 1986 Vienna Convention on the Law of Treaties between States and International Organizations or between International Organizations. For a broader definition see P. Reuter, *Introduction to the Law of Treaties*, p. 23, London/New York, St Martin, 1989.

13. Text of the 23 October 1991 Agreements in the United Nations and Cambodia 1991–95, pp. 132–48, New York, United Nations, 1995.

14. Text of the General Framework Agreement of Dayton, 21 November, and Paris, 14 December 1995, *Review of International Affairs*, Belgrade, 16 February 1996. Concerning the problem of the nature of the conflict as international or non-international, see the discussion by G. Aldrich, 'Jurisdiction of the International Criminal Tribunal for the Former Yugoslavia', *American Journal of International Law*, 1996, pp. 64–9.

15. See P. Gaeta, 'The Dayton Agreements and International Law', *European Journal of International Law*, 1996, pp. 147–63. The accord consists of a set of agreements. First, there is a General Framework Agreement, a treaty concluded by the Republic of Bosnia and Herzegovina, the Republic of Croatia and the Federal Republic of Yugoslavia and guaranteeing the rest, then comes a series of annexed agreements concluded mainly by Bosnia and Herzegovina and the two entities directly involved in the conflict (which are not parties to the General Framework Agreement).

that the other agreements examined here are international treaties in the sense either of the 1969 or 1986 Vienna Conventions, or even in the most informal way the International Court of Justice has handled the legal nature of an international agreement in the Aegean Sea Continental Shelf Case (1978). The judgement has stressed that, in the case of an international instrument of disputed nature 'in determining what was indeed the nature of the act or transaction . . . the Court must have regard above all to its actual terms and to the particular circumstances in which it was drawn up'.[16] Peace agreements concluded to end civil wars are not of this kind, mainly because the parties to them are neither states nor international organizations.

Nevertheless, international law has known for at least the last fifty years important agreements that were not considered treaties. These were known, along with day-to-day arrangements of minimal importance, as gentleman's agreements.[17] But the concept of gentleman's agreements could not embrace everything of a non-conventional character. Because of the magnitude of the commitments envisaged by the agreements in question, the doctrine was induced to speak of 'purely political agreements' or 'non-binding agreements'.[18] This category of acts includes fragile international agreements, which are submitted to the principle *rebus sic stantibus,* rather than to the principle *pacta sunt servanda.* Changing circumstances can influence the attitude of states parties to ignore their commitments without engaging their international responsibility and without opening the door to international arbitration or judicial settlement. Can we classify intrastate peace agreements under this heading as purely political or non-binding agreements? Besides the fact that the 'category' as such is still

---

16. *ICJ Reports 1978*, p. 40, para. 96.
17. Robert Y. Jennings, 'The Treaties', in M. Bedjaoui (ed.), *International Law: Achievements and Prospects*, p. 135, Paris/Dordrecht/Boston/London, UNESCO/Martinus Nijhoff Publishers, 1991.
18. See M. Virally, '[La distinction entre] textes internationaux de portée juridique et textes internationaux dépourvus de portée juridique', *Annuaire de l'Institut de droit international (Cambridge Session)*, Vol. 60, No. 1, 1983, pp. 166–374; R. R. Baxter, 'International Law in Her Infinite Variety', *International and Comparative Law Quarterly*, 1980, pp. 557 et seq.; O. Schachter, *International Law in Theory and Practice*, pp. 84–105, Dordrecht/Boston/London, 1991.

Peace agreements as   119
instruments for
the resolution of
intrastate conflicts

challenged,[19] in the sense that international law cannot shelter them (a treaty is a treaty, is a treaty, etc.),[20] we should answer in the negative for another reason: in effect, purely political or non-binding agreements are a luxury of interstate relations. If they are weak in terms of legal intensity at the outset, they can, nevertheless, be promoted to international treaties under the conditions indicated by the International Court of Justice in the aforementioned case. The commitments undertaken by a given instrument might be qualified as political or legal, but this does not impair the fact that states are always bound by the wide web of general international (customary) law, which determines the framework of their behaviour internationally.

The agreements purporting to establish peace in the wake of civil conflict are certainly subject to the intricacies of the *rebus sic stantibus* axiom, since they operate under extremely fragile and volatile conditions. However, this in no way negates the fundamental binding element they include as a presumption, namely, that the clauses agreed upon will be honoured. The duty to abide by one's word constitutes today a general rule of the law of civilized nations and, in this specific case, we may be able to speak of 'non-treaty *pacta sunt servanda*'. Thus the contracting parties are bound by the agreement, on the one hand because they concluded it, and on the other because the agreement also contains clauses the non-respect of which violates rules of international law on the maintenance of international peace and security of pivotal importance for the United Nations.

As said before, peace agreements in intrastate conflicts are neither treaties nor 'purely political' or 'non-binding' agreements. However, even in the text of interstate non-binding agreements such as the documents of the Conference (now Organization) on Security and Co-operation in Europe, rules which are included in these documents are binding 'otherwise': either the rules stem from general (customary) international law, or they are obligatory for some or all of the parties because they are included in international instruments of a legally binding

---

19. The problem of the normative relativity is thoroughly discussed by P. Weil, 'Le droit international en quête de son identité', *Recueil des Cours de l'Académie de droit international de La Haye*, 1992 (VI), pp. 52 et seq.

20. See on this subject the article by M. Halberstam in *Virginia Journal of International Law*, 1992, pp. 51 et seq.

character. We have tried to describe this situation by using the term 'trans-textuality'.[21]

The conclusion is that in all agreements, whatever their legal nature, there are provisions legally binding 'otherwise'. If the document is a treaty, the already existing rule is consolidated, confirmed or refined. First, in our case of internal conflict, it is extremely hazardous to pretend that the peace agreements in question are submitted to domestic law. Indeed, insurgency and civil war either cause domestic public law and order to collapse, or make it inoperative. Second, in such a case by definition domestic institutions are also to be redefined; thus the commitments undertaken cannot rely upon a state apparatus and law that have proved to be unworkable. Third, the internal armed conflict has already put in motion rules of international law that are taken over, confirmed and individualized by the accord. Consequently, it is inconceivable to say that in the phase of achieving peace it suffices that the agreement is either to be submitted to domestic law, or to a choice of law or to nothing.

THE CONCEPT OF TRANS-TEXTUALITY

Under the general concept of 'trans-textuality', we must now also include the case in which the peace agreement terminating the internal conflict forms part of the United Nations procedures and leads to the use of powers under the provisions of the United Nations Charter which aim at the preservation and restoration of international peace and security (including 'measures' under Chapter VII of the Charter), thus constituting a peculiar 'accord' situated within the ambit of binding rules of international law.

Leaving apart the questions of maintenance of international peace and security, the formal deficiencies of an intrastate peace agreement are often remedied by its endorsement by the Security Council. Hence the agreement becomes an act of the international organization and operates as such towards the

---

21.   E. Roucounas, 'Remarques sur la portée juridique des engagements CSCE concernant la dimension humaine', in E. Decaux and L.-A. Sicilianos (eds.), *La CSCE: Dimension humaine et règlement des différends*, pp. 105–8, Paris, Centre de Droit International de Paris X-Nanterre, Montchrestien, 1993.

Peace agreements as 121
instruments for
the resolution of
intrastate conflicts

parties and towards the international community as a whole. In any case, at the conclusion of the agreement the parties express their consent to the participation of the United Nations in the implementation of the instrument and formally invite the United Nations to act accordingly.[22] The Security Council, in its much commented summit meeting of 31 January 1992, underlined that

United Nations peace-keeping tasks have increased and broadened considerably in recent years. Election monitoring, human rights verification and the repatriation of refugees have in the settlement of some regional conflicts, at the request or with the agreement of the parties concerned, been integral parts of the Security Council's efforts to maintain international peace and security.[23]

These agreements are not only non-treaties, but also in most cases, as regards their contents, depart from what is traditionally regulated by peace treaties. Furthermore, they are not only armistice agreements,[24] as they tend both to end the conflict in all its components and also to organize the future. As a general remark, their military clauses are intimately linked to the clauses on the foundation of peace. The instrument seeks, even if it actually does not succeed, a comprehensive settlement of the conflict.

THE CONTENTS OF PEACE TREATIES BETWEEN STATES

In order to form an idea of the differences between the peace agreements in question and peace treaties concluded between states,[25] we shall briefly recall the

---

22. The peace agreements include clauses of acceptance by the parties of the role of the international community and especially of the United Nations in monitoring and guaranteeing the implementation of each agreement. See, for example, B. Boutris-Ghali, 'Introduction', *The United Nations and Mozambique 1992–1995*, p. 19, New York, United Nations, 1995.
23. UN Doc. S/23500, 31 January 1992, p. 2.
24. The evolutive character of this notion is stressed by Y. Dinstein, 'Armistice', in R. Bernhardt (ed.), *Encyclopedia of International Law*, pp. 31 et seq., Instalment No. 3.
25. See Sir G. Fitzmaurice, 'The Juridical Clauses of Peace Treaties', *Recueil des Cours de l'Académie de droit international de La Haye*, 1948 (II), pp. 255 et seq.; W. G. Grewe, 'Peace Treaties', in *Encyclopedia of International Law*, op. cit., pp. 192 et seq., Instalment No. 4; E. von Puttkamer, 'Peace Treaties of 1947', ibid., pp. 117 et seq.; W. Morvay, 'Peace Treaty with Japan (1951)', ibid., pp. 125 et seq.

main features of the latter. Obviously, in the first place, peace treaties deal with the termination of all hostilities and in this point they coincide with the contents of peace agreements. But, for the rest, the objects of their provisions differ in many respects. Peace treaties contain first and foremost political and territorial clauses in which questions of cession of territory, boundaries, relations with neighbouring states, plebiscites, minorities, restrictions imposed on the armed forces of the defeated powers, disarmament, dismantling and removal of their industrial equipment, reparations, fate of pre-war private contracts, financial and commercial arrangements prevail.

Then follows a series of guarantee clauses, including military occupation by the victors, neutralization and demilitarization. Finally, disputes arising out of the application and interpretation of certain provisions of these treaties are often referred to mixed claims commissions and, in some cases, to the International Court of Justice. It should also be noted that the post-Second World War peace treaties were not so well structured as the post-First World War peace treaties in matters of human rights (minorities).[26] In the following paragraphs we shall see that the peace agreements negotiated at the instigation of the United Nations and/or other international organizations and individual interested states, differ fundamentally in their structure, contents and follow-up from what has been until now the formula for guaranteeing a lasting peace at the end of an international conflict. In some respects, the differentiation is due not so much to the international character of the conflict as to the changing conceptions about the establishment of peace in general.

The problem of the quality of the parties

The international legislators, strongly preoccupied by the protection of all persons on humanitarian grounds during armed conflicts of any nature, were anxious to circumvent the problem of the quality, international legal personality and recognition of the parties. They did so in the aforementioned international

---

26.   See St. Verosta, 'Peace Treaties after World War I', *Encyclopedia of International Law*, op. cit., Instalment No. 4, pp. 110 et seq.

Peace agreements as   123
instruments for
the resolution of
intrastate conflicts

humanitarian instruments of 1949 and 1977.[27] The problem emerges in the most acute and difficult way when negotiations and a settlement are in sight. No international rule can be referred to automatically. The government in place, which is keen to eliminate any presumption of recognition of the 'other party', constantly and in every respect challenges its status, name and representation. Naturally, the 'other party' works for the opposite. Sometimes, as happened with the 1968 Paris Peace Talks on Viet Nam the problem arises even of how to sit at the negotiating table. In that case, the settlement of the question took a good number of months. Similar are issues of negotiations taking place directly or indirectly between the parties, with 'proximity' or not. For the United Nations this is an old and real problem indeed.[28] In the late 1940s, in the first conciliatory procedures engaged by the Organization, the revolutionary parties were, for political reasons, anxious to gain formal recognition by the United Nations. Since then, every imaginable expression has been put forward in order to overcome this obstacle and enter into the phase of substantial negotiation of the conditions of peace. Even today, some revolutionary or liberation movements are called by one name by themselves, differently by the United Nations and by another name by the government in place. It is recalled that on one occasion, when the revolutionaries were pressing a United Nations mediator to clarify their international status, they finally declared they were satisfied by his following answer: 'You are what you are.'[29]

---

27. See Y. Sandoz, C. Swinarski and B. Zimmermann (eds.), *Commentary on the Additional Protocols of 8 June 1977 to the Geneva Conventions of 12 August 1949*, pp. 1362 et seq., Geneva, International Committee of the Red Cross, 1987.
28. M.-C. Bourloyannis-Vrailas, 'The Convention on the Safety of United Nations and Associated Personnel', *International and Comparative Law Quarterly*, 1995, pp. 560 et seq., reports that, during the elaboration of the Convention on the Protection of United Nations Personnel in Peace-keeping Operations (1993/94), the Nordic countries proposed the insertion of a provision authorizing the participation of non-state entities to the Convention by a unilateral declaration of acceptance. Although it was clearly stated that this would not in any way affect the status of the entities in question, the proposal was rejected.
29. From the author's interview (1963) with United Nations mediator Franck Graham.

Who signs? Parties and witnesses

The standard form of signature of peace agreements includes, along with the representatives of the parties, that of a representative of the United Nations (special representative of the Secretary-General in place, or his envoy). This has been the case for El Salvador and Guatemala. The Guatemala City Agreement of 29 December 1996 bears the signature of the parties and of Boutros Boutros-Ghali, the Secretary-General of the United Nations.[30] In other situations the document also bears the signatures of the Secretary-General or of a representative of the regional organization involved in the peace process (in Rwanda, the Secretary-General of the Organization of African Unity, in Bosnia and Herzegovina, the Representative of the European Union). The accords are signed 'in presence', but without the signature, of representatives of observer states (in the case of Angola, the United States, the Russian Federation and Portugal).[31] In the case of Bosnia and Herzegovina, the accords were 'witnessed' by means of their signature by representatives of the European Union, the United States, the Russian Federation, Germany, the United Kingdom and France. In other cases, the international mediators involved in the negotiation also sign the document.[32] The Declaration and Agreement between the Russian Federation and the Chechnya Republic of 30 August 1996 was signed in presence of the head of the Assistance Group of the Organization for Co-operation and Security in Europe (OSCE). In Mozambique the accord was also signed by the representatives of the Government of Italy, and the religious authorities of the country. The peace settlement for Cambodia was embodied in a Final Act of the Paris Conference and was signed by the four Cambodian parties and by the co-chairmen of the Conference (France and Indonesia). It contained a series of instruments signed by the representatives of the participating states to the Paris Conference and included an agreement on a comprehensive political settlement of the Cambodia conflict (in one of whose

---

30. See UN Doc. S/1977/114, p. 40; UN Doc. A/51/796.
31. See UN Doc. S/1994/1141 (Lusaka Protocol of 15 November 1994).
32. In the case of Mozambique, see the Agreement of 4 October 1992 signed at San Egidio, Rome, in *the United Nations and Mozambique*, supra note 22, at p. 123.

Peace agreements as   125
instruments for
the resolution of
intrastate conflicts

annexes 'the parties' are the Cambodian political parties, not all signatories) and an agreement concerning the sovereignty, independence, territorial integrity, inviolability, neutrality and national unity of Cambodia. Finally, no text concerning the civil war and the breakdown of the state in Somalia can be qualified as a peace agreement: the conflict was dealt with by the international community mainly on the basis of a number of relevant resolutions and decisions of the United Nations Security Council.[33]

The preliminary instruments

The conclusion of a peace agreement is generally preceded by a number of preliminary instruments of unequal importance which lead to the conclusion of the main (or final) agreement. Sometimes the parties conclude a 'framework agreement' which is in itself as binding as the final agreement. In the case of Cambodia, the comprehensive settlement of 1991 was based on a 'framework document' of 1990, unanimously endorsed by the Security Council.[34]

Main features

As we have said, each case presents specific characteristics that have to be dealt with carefully taking into consideration the particularities it addresses and the situation in the field. This is one of the reasons why there is no model peace agreement for intrastate conflicts. However, the weakness of the case-by-case approach to peaceful settlement is that it creates serious difficulties for the Secretary-General and the United Nations mission in charge of the follow-up of the agreement, and it continuously complicates the task of the United Nations as a whole.[35]

---

33. See Y. Osinbajo, 'Legality in a Collapsed State: The Somalia Experience', *International and Comparative Law Quarterly*, 1996, pp. 910 et seq.
34. *The United Nations and Cambodia 1991–1995*, New York, 1995, p. 135. See also Akashi, op. cit., supra note 11. As for Central America, see S/RES/637 of 27 July 1989.
35. See E. Bertram, 'Reinventing Governments. The Promise and Perils of United Nations Peace Building', *Journal of Conflict Resolution*, 1995, pp. 387 et seq.

Peace agreements contain strict, definite provisions on timetables and deadlines for the parties to dismantle revolutionary or rebel forces, reduce the size of government forces,[36] repatriate refugees,[37] promulgate legislation, set up mechanisms of protection of human rights, organize free elections, etc.[38] (in the case of Rwanda, Article 7 of the 3 August 1993 Arusha Agreement required implementation of certain provisions in thirty-seven days!).[39] In practice, the very firm provisions are constantly postponed and modified. New deadlines are negotiated, until the happy moment of complete implementation of the agreement (itself also modified in some of its substantial provisions) finally arrives.

Another element that must be borne in mind is that in almost all cases there is no single instrument for the settlement of the conflict. Usually the implementers have to face a situation in which there is a main agreement (or two or three main agreements),[40] accompanied by some separate declarations, protocols, lists, plans, maps, etc., signed the same day. This main act is supplemented by an unlimited number of subsequent documents, correspondence, explanatory notes, reports established by one or by all the parties, and more frequently by United Nations representatives and missions in charge of the verification of implementation of the

---

36. And the withdrawal of foreign forces (Mozambique, Angola, Cambodia).
37. *The United Nations and Rwanda 1993–1996*, Doc. 19, p. 191, New York, United Nations, 1996.
38. See for Mozambique, *The United Nations and Mozambique*, op. cit., pp. 118 et seq. and 122 et seq. For El Salvador, *The United Nations and El Salvador*, pp. 23 et seq., New York, United Nations, 1995, and Annex II, Caracas, 21 May 1990, p. 117.
39. See ibid., Doc. 19 on transitional institutions, p. 171.
40. For the recent peace settlement (Guatemala), the long list of agreements is as follows: 30 March 1990 (Oslo Agreement); 26 April 1991 (Agreement on the Procedure for the Search for Peace by Political Means); 25 July 1991 (Querétano Agreement); 19 January 1994 (Framework Agreement); 19 April 1994 (Comprehensive Agreement on Human Rights); 19 April 1994 (Agreement on a Timetable); 1 July 1994 (Agreement on the Resettlement of the Population Groups Uprooted by the Armed Conflict); 1 July 1994 (Agreement on the Establishment of the Commission to Clarify Human Rights Violations); 10 April 1995 (Agreement on the Indigenous Peoples); 6 June 1996 (Agreement on Social and Economic Aspects and Agrarian Situation); 16 October 1995 (Agreement on the Strenghtening of the Civilian Power and on the Role of Armed Forces in a Democratic Society); 29 December 1996 (Agreements of Guatemala City 'on a firm lasting peace', UN Doc.S/1997/114, A/51/796 of 7 February 1997.

Peace agreements as
instruments for
the resolution of
intrastate conflicts   127

main agreement. Then come the relevant reports of the Secretary-General and the resolutions of the Security Council and the General Assembly. All these acts are of primary importance, as they endorse the agreed terms of peace, without excluding the possibility of inducing, in the course of action, slight or blunt modifications of the letter and spirit of the main agreement.

It also happens that the peace settlement is not based on a single agreement. Either the implementation of one agreement reveals insufficiencies and lacunae that necessitate the conclusion of new agreements regulating the remaining issues, or the parties, by resorting to a step-by-step process, arrive by a series of sectoral commitments to the conclusion of peace. In such a case, the totality of the accords concluded during the long negotiation must be taken into account, and there is no superseding document to be considered as the definitive one.[41] Only rarely does a new agreement encapsulate the entire settlement and absorb the totality of the provisions arrived at by the parties during the different phases of the peace process.

In a more general sense, it must be recalled that in the framework of the United Nations resolutions and decisions the axiom *lex posterior derogat priori* is not a functional one. Indeed, all United Nations resolutions and decisions are supposed to remain in force until they have lost their object or are expressly set aside by subsequent acts of the same organ that adopted them.

A number of peace agreements contain elaborate provisions on the matters they regulate (Rwanda, El Salvador), others not (Haiti, Guatemala). Sometimes the axis of interest differs. In Central America the question of human rights and democracy[42] is privileged,[43] whereas in Africa negotiators are keen to establish the rule of law or to set up the main political and security institutions permitting the state to function. In Bosnia and Herzegovina the 1995 Dayton/Paris Agreements

---

41. An early instrument agreed by the parties and welcomed but not endorsed by the Security Council could be considered as a *pactum de contrahendo*. For this notion in international law, see U. Beyerlin, *Encyclopedia of International Law*, Instalment No. 7, p. 371.

42. The Querétaro Agreement S/23256, pp. 10–13.

43. *The United Nations and El Salvador*, op. cit., p. 107. For Cambodia, *United Nations and Cambodia*, op.cit. For Sierra Leone see UN Doc. S/1996/1034, 11 December 1996, Article 19.

provide for almost everything on human rights (they even include a list of twenty-two relevant international treaties in force). A set of constitutional rules is found in the agreements concerning Bosnia and Herzegovina,[44] Cambodia,[45] Rwanda.[46] In general, provisions on fundamental human rights, the role of the armed forces and the police, on political pluralism and political parties, the organization of the judiciary and, first and foremost, the preparation and conduct of free and fair elections are found in all these instruments. As we have said, some agreements also contain model constitutions.

The issue of human rights

All intrastate peace agreements contain specific provisions on the respect of human rights. The important place of this issue in the agreements depends less on the extent to which human rights need to be safeguarded than on the political environment in which the conflict has taken place.[47] In Central America the peace process began with two solemn declarations on human rights. Esquipulas I and Esquipulas II constituted a breakthrough for the peace process in the entire area. In particular, Esquipulas II, signed by the five Central American presidents, opened the way to the cessation of the armed conflict by establishing democracy, decreeing a general amnesty, holding free, pluralistic elections and setting up an International Verification and Follow-up Commission. These two acts led to the establishment of an international on-site mechanism, the United Nations Observer Group in Central America. Subsequently, a series of other instruments

44. Which also contains an Agreement on Inter-Entity Boundary Line and Related Issues.
45. Cambodia, Annex V of the Agreement of 23 October 1991.
46. For Rwanda (see *United Nations and Rwanda*, op. cit., p. 174) the Agreement contains a constitutional framework concerning the executive, the functions of the prime minister and his deputies, the judiciary and rules on 'national ethics'.
47. The short Declaration and List of Principles of 30 August 1996 determining the basis of the mutual relations between the Russian Federation and the Chechnyan Republic make a general reference to the 1948 Universal Declaration of Human Rights and to the 1966 International Covenant on Civil and Political Rights, with emphasis on the right to self-determination, freedom of expression, non-discrimination and commitment for the Chechnyan Republic to enact legislation to this effect. Note also that the agreement directly refers to the application of international law (text translated for the author by Dr E. Klapas).

Peace agreements as   129
instruments for
the resolution of
intrastate conflicts

were adopted: the Declaration of Costa del Sol, where Nicaragua undertook specific commitments, and the participating states expressed readiness to allow the security involvement of the United Nations to expand; the parties to the conflict of El Salvador (the government on the one hand, and the Frente Farabundo Martí para la Liberación Nacional on the other) began the peace dialogue in San José and signed a formal Agreement on Human Rights (1990). In this case we see that the issue of human rights is considered from the outset as an outstanding one which merits a specific document agreed upon by the parties. It is only after the signing of this act that other agreements followed: the Mexico City Agreement envisaged a series of actions aiming at the establishment of a civilian society and provided for the formation of a Commission on Truth to investigate serious violations of human rights.[48] Other truth commissions have been subsequently established with unequal results in several Latin American countries and in South Africa. Thus the peace agreement between the parties to the conflict initiates new United Nations procedures. In the case of El Salvador it led to the creation of the United Nations Observer Mission in El Salvador (ONUSAL), a multifaceted body whose action in the field constitutes a good example of sustained efforts of the international community to bring peace to the war-ravaged country.

A special mention has to be made of clauses guaranteeing in detail the freedom of expression, the free flow of information and the rights of the mass media to function under normal conditions,[49] especially during the electoral period.

The road to democracy

It is perhaps characteristic that in the last decade, if not since the Final Act of Helsinki (1975), intrastate peace agreements necessarily include a chapter on democracy. This attempt to include democracy among the prospects of

48. *United Nations and El Salvador*, op. cit., pp. 37 et seq., 67 et seq. and 290 et seq.
49. *United Nations and Mozambique*, op. cit., p. 109. For Angola, see UN Doc. S/22609, Protocol of Estoril II. For Sierra Leone, Peace Agreement between the Government of the Republic of Sierra Leone and the Revolutionary United Front of Sierra Leone, UN Doc. S/1996/ 1034, 11 December 1996, Article 19, para. 3.

maintaining international peace and security and enhancing development became more intensive after 1988 (Nicaragua). The evolution is impressive, at least on paper. The former United Nations Secretary-General Boutros Boutros-Ghali dedicated two paragraphs to democracy in his *An Agenda for Peace* in 1992[50] and twenty-two paragraphs in his *An Agenda for Development* in 1994.[51] Yet, while the United Nations Charter makes no mention of democracy, the two 1966 International Covenants on Human Rights consider democracy as a bulwark in a second sentence or paragraph indicating exceptions to the enjoyment of only certain rights 'in a democratic society'.[52] Things have changed during the last decade. Today there is no relevant international organization document that does not underline the role of democracy in the establishment of the rule of law, the safeguarding of human rights and the attainment of economic development. There is a strong ideological trend to detect in these documents a rapidly emerging internationally protected right to democratic governance.[53] Obviously, in most cases of peace after an internal conflict, a further transition will be required from democratization to democracy. The former Secretary-General of the United Nations begins his most recent book entitled *An Agenda for Democratization* with the following distinction:

Democratization is a process which leads to a more open, more participatory, less authoritarian society. Democracy is a system of government which embodies, in a variety of institutions and mechanisms, the ideal of political power based on the will of the people.[54]

---

50. UN Doc. A/47/277, United Nations, New York, 1992.
51. UN Doc. A/48/935, United Nations, New York, 1994.
52. Article 21, second sentence; Article 22, para.2. *Inter alia*, the same expression 'in a democratic society' is found in the *European Convention on Human Rights* (1950). The European Court of Human Rights since its judgement in the Handyside Case (1976) regularly recalls that in a democratic society 'pluralism, tolerance and broadmindedness' prevail, while the majority does not abuse its dominant position'.
53. T. Franck, 'The Emerging Right to Democratic Governance', *American Journal of International Law*, 1992, pp. 46 et seq.
54. B. Boutros-Ghali, *An Agenda for Democratization*, p. 1, New York, United Nations, 1996.

Peace agreements as 131
instruments for
the resolution of
intrastate conflicts

Amnesty and pardon

Article 6, paragraph 5, of the 1977 Additional Protocol II to the 1949 Geneva Conventions on humanitarian law contains an interesting element for national reconciliation. It provides that

at the end of the hostilities the parties shall endeavour to grant the broadest possible amnesty to persons who have participated in the armed conflict or those deprived of their liberty for reasons related to the armed conflict, whether they are interned or detained.[55]

These provisions should not lead to misunderstandings. They do not and cannot envisage erasing serious war crimes or crimes against humanity perpetrated during the internal armed conflict[56] by either party or by persons under the jurisdiction and control of the parties.[57] The fact that Protocol II is silent on matters of grave breaches of humanitarian law does not mean that persons committing such breaches are not liable for their acts. The idea of Article 6, paragraph 5, is that peace includes measures of national reconciliation and forgiveness for those who are laying down their arms in order to guarantee a peaceful future for the country. The use of the term 'amnesty' refers to political offences (upheaval, civil conflict, fighting for or against an authoritarian regime). The forgiveness of political offences is sometimes also called a 'pardon' in order to demonstrate the willingness of the victor to act generously, but the term 'pardon' is better suited to individual rather than collective or group situations.

With this explanation it is understandable that the 1996 peace agreement concluded between the Government of the Republic of Sierra Leone and the revolutionary United Front of Sierra Leone provides in Article 14 that:

---

55. Analysis by S. Junod, in Commentary on the Additional Protocols of 8 June 1977 to the Geneva Conventions of 12 August 1949, op. cit., supra note 27, at p. 1402.

56. See T. Meron, 'International Criminalization of Internal Atrocities', *American Journal of International Law*, 1995, pp. 554 et seq.

57. See F. Domb, 'Treatment of War Crimes in Peace Settlements – Prosecution or Amnesty?' in Y. Dinstein and M. Tabory (eds.), *War Crimes in International Law*, pp. 305–20, The Hague/Boston/London, Kluwer AC, 1996.

to consolidate the peace and promote the cause of national reconciliation the Government of Sierra Leone shall ensure that no armed or judicial action is taken against any member of United Front in respect of anything done by them in pursuit of their objectives as members of that organization up to the time of the signing of this Agreement.

In another context, the agreement declares that 'the Parties undertake to respect the principles and rules of humanitarian law'. This formulation reiterates the obvious obligations of the parties to an armed conflict under general (international) humanitarian law, but it also recalls that the rules of humanitarian law extend beyond the mere cessation of hostilities (return of refugees and displaced persons, release of political detainees and prisoners, etc.).

In most but not all peace agreements we find express commitments for national reconciliation through amnesty.[58] Indeed, the problem either continues to exist after the signing of the agreement or occurs later under the popular pressure for fact-finding. Truth commissions were set up in many cases and, by establishing the facts once and for all, they contributed to the elimination of flagrant cases of violation of human rights and helped in the appeasement of public opinion and in building confidence on democratic institutions.

The situation becomes complicated when individuals involved in the perpetration of hideous crimes against humanity, such as the crime of genocide, organized and executed by the government or the revolutionary group to which they belonged, not only have impunity, but also have a role in a government of national reconciliation putting an end to the civil war. Cambodia is the most striking example of such a situation.[59] Whatever the political motivations[60] and whatever the terms of a written or unwritten agreement concluded between the

---

58. For Haiti, the Governors Island Peace Agreement of 3 July 1993, para. 6, UN Doc. S/26063, 12 July 1993. On the problem of Haiti in general, see Y. Daudet (ed.), *La Crise d'Haïti (1991–1996)*, Paris, Cahiers Internationaux, Montchrestien, 1996.

59. See S. Marks, 'Forgetting the "Policies and Practices of the Past". Impunity in Cambodia', *The Fletcher Forum of World Affairs*, 1994, pp. 17 et seq.

60. See J. P. Langellier, 'Armistice, génocide et raison d'État', *Le Monde* (Paris), 26 September 1996, p. 1.

parties, the personal criminal responsibility for such crimes cannot be wiped out by amnesty measures. There are *erga omnes* crimes under international law[61] where all states must co-operate in order to arrest, prosecute or extradite the offenders for trial and punishment.

All intrastate peace agreements contain arrangements concerning the return of exiles and the release of political prisoners and detainees and, as the case might be, of prisoners of war. The discussion on the qualification of each particular case on the basis of an agreed (or not agreed) definition of detention is another difficult issue entrusted to international supervision. The task of identifying political detainees from among common detainees usually belongs to an 'independent jurist' who is nominated by the Secretary-General of the United Nations and who, among other tasks, offers his services to this effect. When the parties are politically and psychologically ready to go along with this question, the humanitarian operation is successful. Up to now, the best example of such co-operation between the parties and United Nations agents has been in Namibia.

Organization of the judiciary

Restricting the powers of state armed forces or disarming rebels and transforming revolutionary movements into political parties is not adequate. Nor does it suffice to train urgently the entire state mechanism and the population as a whole to respect human rights. The organization of the judiciary constitutes one of the most difficult phases in the process of implementation of peace accords. It is not possible to talk about the rule of law without the minimum guarantees for the independence of the judiciary, without its proper separation from the state

---

61. Article VI of Annex 7 of the 1995 Dayton/Paris Agreement on Bosnia and Herzegovina, in line with the Statute of the International Criminal Tribunal for the former Yugoslavia, reserves from the measure of amnesty 'serious violations of humanitarian international law'. See J. R. D. W. Jones, 'The Implications of the Peace Agreement for the International Criminal Tribunal', *European Journal of International Law*, 1996, pp. 233–4; D. Shrag and R. Zacklin, 'The International Criminal Tribunal for the Former Yugoslavia', *European Journal of International Law*, 1994, pp. 360 et seq.; idem, 'The International Criminal Tribunal for Rwanda', *European Journal of International Law*, 1996, pp. 501 et seq.

executive authority mechanisms and without reforming the penal code and criminal procedure. It must also be noted that, in many cases, the verification by international organs of the unsoundness of the judiciary caused the same judiciary to reject such findings, though it may not wish to renew its practices. In Central America, in 1994, research conducted by a human-rights institute showed that public opinion continued to hold in rather low esteem the armed forces, politicians and the judiciary, while it greatly esteemed electoral courts. It is worth pointing out that the latter do not constitute new court institutions but rather old formations which have now the fortitude to rally to the requirements for transition to a democratic society.

The weakest link: agricultural reform, landownership, economic development

Peace agreements express gratitude to foreign governments willing to contribute to the restoration of peace through economic means. Sometimes the accords contain plans for economic restructuring and growth, provide for the return of land to its owners,[62] for land reform, and include firm commitments from the government to organize the economy[63] on the basis of free-market models.

These provisions are rather programmatory and risk remaining in the area of wishful thinking if they are not supported by outside aid. But we can hardly find a single peace agreement in which the 'witnessing' representatives of foreign developed states formally bind their governments to come to the assistance of the pacified country.

---

62.   *United Nations and El Salvador*, op. cit., pp. 161 and 555.
63.   Articles 6 to 9 of the 1996 Guatemala City Agreement for a firm and lasting peace deals with socio-economic problems and their solution (UN Doc. S/1997/114). The 1996 Peace Agreement on Sierra Leone provides in Article 26 for the creation of a 'National Socio-Economic Forum' (UN.Doc. 1996/1034).

Peace agreements as 135
instruments for
the resolution of
intrastate conflicts

Preparation and carrying out of free and fair elections

All the provisions of peace agreements culminate in the organization of free elections.[64] 'E-Day' is the most sensitive moment of the peace process. Agreements between the parties and the preparation (sometimes including pressure from the United Nations, regional organizations and foreign states) fall into three equally important phases of the electoral process which require different actions: the period before the elections, the election itself (elections being qualified as the true birth of democracy)[65] and the 'day after'. A delicate path is that of the transformation of revolutionary movements into political parties by integrating them into civilian life.[66] Another extremely complicated issue is that of electoral registration. In at least one case this issue could prove fatal for the whole implementation of the peace agreement.

INTERNATIONAL MONITORING OF PEACE-BUILDING

In the implementation of all peace agreements there is also a strong presence of the international community. With the exception of some conflicts in the former Soviet Union, the United Nations are present in all the inextricable baskets of relevant actions and in conditions put down or not referred to by the agreements themselves. This is a new United Nations activity, called 'peace-building'. As Boutros Boutros-Ghali explained in his *An Agenda for Peace*:

Preventive diplomacy seeks to resolve disputes before violence breaks out; peace-making and peace-keeping are required to halt conflicts and preserve peace once it is obtained. If

---

64. On this capital question see K. Vasak, *Freedom of Election and the International Observation of Elections*, Tricontinental Institute of Parliamentary Democracy, University of La Laguna, Spain, 1994; H. Gros Espiell, 'Liberté des élections et observation internationale des élections', ibid.; G. S. Goodwin Gill, *Élections libres et régulières. Droit international et pratique*, Geneva, 1994, p. 29; Y. Beigbeder, *International Monitoring of Plebiscites, Referenda and National Elections. Self-determination and Transition to Democracy*, Dordrecht/Boston/London, 1994.

65. Vasak, op. cit., p. 15.

66. See criteria and arrangements for the formation and recognition of political parties in the Agreement on Mozambique, supra note 22 at p. 107.

successful, they strengthen the opportunity for post-conflict peace-building, which can prevent the recurrence of violence among nations and peoples.[67]

Usually the United Nations is present in the field with two components, one military and one political ('you need the military dimension to keep [the two sides] apart and the political to get them together').[68] Furthermore, the terms of reference of the United Nations agents in charge are sometimes modified in order either to meet the needs of changing situations (by strengthening the military or the political branch according to circumstances) or to confirm in diplomatic terms the failure of the international organization to make possible the implementation of the agreements.

The United Nations is not and could not be alone in the effort to assist parties in implementing peace agreements. Other international organizations as well as non-governmental organizations rush to the field. They contribute by their political weight and by their skilful personnel to the attainment of the same goal. However, experience shows that better co-ordination is always needed and that questions of prestige or politics can impede the exercise. Speaking of co-ordination, a Council of Europe expert has recently pinpointed in the 1995 Dayton/Paris Peace Agreements on Bosnia and Herzegovina, eleven procedures of monitoring, by different international organizations, in a single clause of these agreements.

Lastly, a word of praise and gratitude is due to all the courageous international agents, men and women, who, away from their homes and families and living under harsh conditions of psychology, climate and security, accomplish in the field the noble mission of serving peace.

One of the greatest successes of the United Nations has been the eradication of apartheid.[69] After the long combats of the African people, South Africa and Namibia entered the normalization phase in the late 1980s. In the case of South Africa, the National Peace Accord of 1991[70] was the basis for the institutional and

67. B. Boutros-Ghali, *An Agenda for Peace*, pp. 11–12, New York, United Nations, 1992.
68. Cited by Bertram, op. cit., p. 396.
69. See *The United Nations and Apartheid 1948–1994*, New York, United Nations, 1994.
70. Ibid., op. cit., pp. 323 et seq.

Peace agreements as 137
instruments for
the resolution of
intrastate conflicts

constitutional reforms in the country as well as for national reconciliation.[71] For Namibia,[72] a series of international treaties, concluded from 1988 onwards, provided for and succeeded in the effective application of Security Council Resolution 435/1978 (on independence). The Namibia Agreements were international treaties which were guaranteed by the Security Council.[73] However, in both cases South Africa as well as Namibia, the mediation of the United Nations, with the consent of the parties, and the creation of special international organs of assistance, observation and verification were crucial in the normalization process.

LEGITIMIZATION

In principle, the completion of the electoral process brings the parties to the status of legitimization.[74] The mere fact that elections have been organized and held under fair conditions opens the way to the establishment of a democratic regime and to the legitimization of all parties that contributed to this end. Be it first-time elections or transitional elections, the international community is present in the process through observers and other specialists of electoral procedures and monitoring. These international agents convey their findings to the Secretary-General of the United Nations, and to other international organizations and officials, and their assessment is of crucial importance for the fate of the contending parties. The behaviour of the parties during and after the electoral process is a key to their legitimization. The defeated party that refuses to acknowledge the genuine electoral result (as happened in Angola) and continues to challenge the new political situation in the country loses any recognition by the

71. See, *inter alia*, the document Republic of South Africa, Promotion of National Unity and Reconciliation Bill, Ministry of Justice, No. B 30-1995.
72. See G. Abi-Saab, 'Namibia and International Law', *African Yearbook of International Law*, 1993, pp. 3 et seq.; M. Singela, 'The Role of the United Nations Transition Assistance Group in the Independence Process of Namibia', ibid., pp. 13 et seq.
73. See C. Cadoux, 'Vers la création prochaine d'un État de Namibie', *Annuaire français de droit international*, 1988, pp. 13–36, at p. 22.
74. See E. Theuermann, 'Legitimizing Governments through International Verification: The Role of the United Nations', *Austrian Journal of Public International Law*, 1995, pp. 129 et seq.

United Nations, whereas the other party or parties have the right of collective protection and assistance. Thus, legitimization is, after the cessation of hostilities, a most important consequence of the full implementation of the peace accord. However, this situation is not exempt from the danger of the government, once the election is over and the international community ceases to exercise pressure, to relapse into authoritarian practices.[75] Under present conditions there is no international system guaranteeing the permanent legitimization of governments.

CONCLUDING REMARKS

This 'new' category of peace agreements or accords in intrastate conflicts constitutes the key to a critical and decisive transition. If, for many reasons, it is not strong in itself, it must be further strengthened, with the assistance of international organizations and interested states, by procedures and means preventing resumption of hostilities and aiming at the establishment of a lasting peace in the country.

We can argue at length on the legal nature of these instruments. There is certainly a first difficulty as to the status of the parties, which according to the case in hand may be qualified as nearer or further away from the concept of 'international legal personality'. But in this chapter we have tried to draw the attention to the fact that irrespective of the legal quality of the parties and whatever the foundation of their binding character, these agreements invariably enter the universe of trans-textuality. By that we mean that their provisions either meet rules guaranteed by general international law and by legal instruments of universal acceptance and/or are framed within acts of the United Nations and thus mobilize competences of peace-keeping and peace-building of the United Nations and regional organizations.

On the other hand, their essential feature is that they are assisted agreements. In addition to the parties to the conflict who have obviously reached the decision to live together in peace, the intervention of third parties both in the formation

---

75.   M. Goulding, 'The Evolution of United Nations Peace-keeping', *International Affairs*, 1993, p. 451.

Peace agreements as 139
instruments for
the resolution of
intrastate conflicts

and adoption, as well as in the interpretation and implementation of these accords, is continuous and pressing. The existence of such accords certainly corresponds to contemporary aspirations for a better world, and forms part of a more comprehensive understanding of international peace. The third party ('non-party') intervenors are first and foremost the United Nations and regional organizations. But a pivotal role is always played by the permanent members of the Security Council or by some of them.[76] If these powers were not to show an active interest in the settlement of the dispute then the intervention of the international organization, loudly pronounced in the text of all such agreements, would constantly prove inadequate, not so much in the formation of the accords but in their implementation.

As to the content of these agreements, their basic characteristic is that they always aim, by different means but through the conduct of free elections, at the establishment of the rule of law through further procedural guarantees for the respect of human rights. Indeed, a meeting of minds after the recent political developments in the world, shows how quickly the international community is moving away from the old doctrine of non-intervention (perhaps without a clear idea of what the 'new' doctrine is) in the domestic affairs of a state. Furthermore, we are witnessing a more articulated approach of the principle, cherished for many years, endorsed by the 1970 General Assembly Declaration on the Principles of International Law Governing Friendly Relations and Co-operation among States in Accordance with the Charter of the United Nations (Resolution 2625 (XXI)) and recalled at least twice by the International Court of Justice in 1975[77] and 1986,[78] that states (or peoples) have the right freely to choose the

---

76. See, for example, L. Melvern, 'The United Nations in Rwanda', *London Review of Books*, 14 December 1996, pp. 11–13; F. Ouguergouz, 'La tragédie rwandaise du printemps 1994: quelques considérations sur les premières réactions de l'Organisation des Nations Unies', *Revue générale de droit international public*, 1996, pp. 149 et seq.

77. Opinion on Western Sahara, *ICJ Reports 1975*, para. 95: 'No rule of international law, in the view of the Court, requires the structure of a State to follow any particular pattern, as is evident from the diversity of the forms of State found in the world today.'

78. Military and para-military activities in and against Nicaragua. Merits. Judgement, *ICJ Reports 1986*, para. 258: 'Every State possesses a fundamental right to choose and implement its own political, economic and social systems.'

political, social and economic regime of their preference.[79] The current version of such a freedom is that states and peoples choose, but within the framework of the rule of law. Although this framework is not very precise, it at least retains the generally recognized fundamental rules on human rights. Democracy should constitute the result of the process. And peace accords must be part and parcel of this reasoning.

Thus in most cases, whereas thanks to these agreements civil war is over, peace through democracy has a long way to go. This latter difficulty is not particular to states that are victims of a civil conflict. The same situation is met by a number of other states all over the world. And the question is whether the United Nations has indeed acquired (besides the need for full support by the Security Council and the co-operation of each of its permanent members) the necessary infrastructure that would effectively contribute to the peace process at large.

---

79. R. Ben Achour, 'Égalité souveraine des États, droit des peuples à disposer d'eux-mêmes et liberté de choix du système politique, économique, culturel et social', in *Liber Amicorum Federico Mayor*, Vol. II, pp. 787 et seq., Brussels, 1995.

Regional arrangements and conflict resolution in Latin America

Antonio Augusto Cançado Trindade

The domain of peaceful resolution of international conflicts appears marked by the ineluctable and persistent ambivalence between, on the one hand, states' general duty of peaceful settlement and, on the other, the freedom of choice accorded to them as to the means of settlement to be employed. The inherent tension between the general duty of peaceful resolution and the free choice of means has had repercussions in the application of international instruments. Conflict resolution remains particularly vulnerable to manifestations of state voluntarism and considerations of accommodation of power, thereby resisting attempts at codification or systematization.[1]

Despite that, multiple instruments of conflict resolution have been devised and applied in the last decades, with varying results. A study of the matter cannot disregard the nature of the disputes. Most of the conflicts that come to mind are those between two or more states, that is, those that fall within the norms of

---

1.   Thus, it has on occasions been relegated to jurisdictional clauses appearing in optional protocols, rather than in the codification conventions themselves. For a criticism, see H. W. Briggs, 'The Optional Protocols of Geneva (1958) and Vienna (1961, 1963) Concerning the Compulsory Settlement of Disputes', *Recueil d'études de Droit international en hommage à Paul Guggenheim*, Geneva, IUHEI, 1968, pp. 628–41; S. Rosenne, 'The Settlement of Treaty Disputes under the Vienna Convention of 1969', *Zeitschrift für ausländisches öffentliches Recht und Völkerrecht*, Vol. 31, 1971, pp. 1–62; R. J. Dupuy, 'Codification et règlement des différends – Les débats de Vienne sur les procédures de règlement', *Annuaire français de droit international*, Vol. 15, 1969, pp. 70–90.

public international law. But there are also conflicts between individuals or private groups and states, in distinct contexts and areas of human activity. Furthermore, there have been means of conflict resolution that have operated at global (United Nations) level, and those that have functioned at regional level. In the present chapter we shall survey the experience accumulated in Latin American arrangements on conflict resolution, with special attention to disputes between two or more states.

RESOLUTION OF INTERSTATE CONFLICTS

Prior to the systematization of peaceful settlement of international disputes undertaken by the 1948 American Treaty of Peaceful Settlement (Pact of Bogotá), arbitration was seldom contemplated and concretized in the practice of some Latin American states.[2] The mechanism of (multilateral) reciprocal consultations (in the case of threats to peace in the region) was created by one of the five instruments adopted by the Inter-American Conference of Buenos Aires in 1936,[3] and was institutionalized shortly afterwards by the Declaration of Lima in 1938. This latter specified that the procedure of consultations would take place through the Meeting of Consultation of Ministers of External Relations.

It should be noted that the organ thus institutionalized in 1938 is the same one that operated continuously in the course of the following decades, and until the 1980s, in the consideration of successive crises such as, for example, in the Anglo-Argentine conflict over the Falklands/Malvinas Islands (1982). By the time the procedure of consultations was created, there was concern with previous treaties which had not yet obtained sufficient ratifications[4] to enter into

---

2.   See, for example, J. J. Caicedo Castilla, 'El arbitraje en las conferencias Panamericanas hasta el Pacto de Bogotá de 1948 sobre soluciones pacíficas', *Boletim da Sociedade Brasileira de Direito Internacional*, Vol. 4, 1948, pp. 5–33.
3.   Namely, the Convention on the Maintenance, Preservation and Re-establishment of Peace.
4.   They were the object of attention of the 1936 Convention to Co-ordinate, Extend and Assure the Fulfilment of Existing Treaties between the American States. This Convention had, as antecedent, the so-called 'Code of Peace' prepared by the Conference of Montevideo of 1933.

force. It was hoped that the launching of the system of reciprocal consultations would henceforth enhance the effectiveness of the procedures of peaceful settlement agreed upon, and consolidate peace on the continent.[5] At the Lima Conference of 1938, it was in fact pointed out that the instruments of conflict prevention on the American continent were dispersed in numerous treaties and declarations, and that it was necessary to co-ordinate them. The much-awaited systemization came with the adoption of the Bogotá Pact of 1948. But despite the latter's contribution at a conceptual level (with, for example, its elaborate definitions of means of settlement),[6] there remained a practical problem. As the pact entered into force through the successive ratifications of the states parties, the effects of previous treaties on peaceful settlement of disputes ceased for these states.[7] But as some states of the region had ratified the pact and others had not, this gave rise to a diversity of situations where individual states were bound either by the Bogotá Pact itself, or by earlier treaties or – as in the case of several Caribbean countries – by none.

The pact was in fact invoked in a boundary conflict between Honduras and Nicaragua in 1957,[8] but this was a rather isolated instance. In the mid-1980s, there remained eighteen member states of the Organization of American states (OAS) that were not subject to the Bogotá Pact. Half of those were bound by earlier treaties,[9] thus forming a rather diversified, if not confusing, framework of international legal instruments for conflict resolution. In addition to that, the lack of ratification by some of its signatories themselves, the denunciation by El Salvador in 1973, the lack of accession by new OAS member states, and the reservations made by some states parties, rendered the pact virtually ineffective.

---

5. C. G. Fenwick, *The Organization of American States*, pp. 182–7, Washington, D.C., Kaufmann, 1963.
6. For a study, see, for example, J. M. Yepes, 'La Conférence Panaméricaine de Bogotá et le droit international américain', *Revue générale de droit international public*, 1949, pp. 52–74.
7. Article LVIII.
8. J. C. Lupinacci, 'Los procedimientos jurisdiccionales en el tratado americano de soluciones pacíficas (Pacto de Bogotá)', *Anuario Uruguayo de Derecho Internacional*, 1962, pp. 205–6.
9. See OAS Document OEA/Ser.G/CP/CAJP-541/84, of 30 July 1984, pp. 80–2.

According to an OAS survey of 1984, only eleven states were bound, in their reciprocal relations, by the procedures of the Bogotá Pact in its entirety.[10] This explains the evolution of the matter in Latin America: it was not surprising to witness, throughout the years, successive calls for ratification of the pact by all OAS member states as the 'best way' to improve and consolidate the regional system of peace,[11] and also to revise the pact.[12] By mid-1999, of the thirty-five member states of the OAS, only fourteen had ratified the pact (three with reservations); with the exception of the Dominican Republic and Haiti, the Caribbean countries have not ratified it.[13]

Given the persistent reluctance of all the states of the region to accept the pact, it is not surprising to find, on reiterated occasions, a search for ad hoc solutions to conflicts outside the institutional mechanisms of the regional system of peace. A clear tendency has developed of favouring the application, instead of a comprehensive codifying instrument such as the Bogotá Pact, of less rigid and more flexible methods of conflict resolution, suitable to each concrete case.[14] Such a reality has persisted until today.

Pertinent examples to this effect are afforded, for example: in Central America, by the handling of the border problem between Costa Rica and Nicaragua in the late 1970s and the conflict between El Salvador and Honduras in

---

10. OAS Document, op. cit., pp. 83–4.
11. OAS General Secretariat, *Comité Jurídico Interamericano, recomendaciones e informes – documentos oficiales 1967–1973*, Vol. 10, pp. 392–407, 1978. *Comité Jurídico Interamericano, recomendaciones e informes – documentos oficiales 1965–1966*, Vol. 9, p. 321, Rio de Janeiro, Gráf. IBGE, 1970.
12. See, for example, César Sepúlveda, 'The Reform of the Charter of the Organization of American States', *Recueil des Cours de l'Académie de droit international*, Vol. 137, 1972, pp. 107–8.
13. Cf. OAS Treaty Series, Nos. 17 and 61 (General Information of the Treaty A-42).
14. F. Orrego Vicuña, 'Análisis de la práctica latinoamericana en materia de solución de controversias durante la década de 1970 y sus implicaciones para el futuro', *Perspectivas del derecho internacional contemporáneo*, Vol. 2, p. 99, Santiago, Universidad de Chile, 1981; Enrique Lagos, 'Los Nuevos mecanismos procesales para la eficacia de la solución pacífica de las controversias, con particular referencia a la práctica de la OEA en los últimos años', *Perspectivas del derecho internacional contemporáneo*, Vol. 2, pp. 79–91, Santiago, Universidad de Chile, 1981.

1980; and, in South America, by the handling of the crisis between Peru and
Ecuador, in the 1980s and 1990s. In Central America, in order to settle border
tensions between Nicaragua and Costa Rica (1977–79), ad hoc fact-finding
commissions were established, and promptly conducted *in loco* observations, and
reported to the OAS Permanent Council. This led to the solution of the conflict,
on an ad hoc basis.[15] As for the conflict between El Salvador and Honduras, it
was settled by the mediation of J. L. Bustamante y Rivero, which led in 1980 to
the treaty of peace between the two countries.[16]

In South America, the prolonged border problem between Ecuador and
Peru, which led to armed confrontation between the two countries in 1981 and
1994/95, was handled invariably by the guarantors designated in the 1942
Protocol of Rio de Janeiro. The Declaration of Peace of Itamaraty, signed by Peru
and Ecuador in Brasilia on 17 February 1995 in the presence of representatives of
the four guarantors, was followed by the Declaration of Montevideo on 28
February of the same year, signed by the foreign ministers of Ecuador and Peru,
together with the foreign ministers of Argentina, Brazil and Chile, and the then
United States Secretary of State, in which they ratified their will to comply fully
with the Declaration of Peace of Itamaraty.

In the Declaration of the Guarantors, signed in Brasilia on 16 April 1997,
they took note of the exchange of the descriptive explanations of the respective
'lists of deadlocks' (*listas de impasses*). They also recalled that it was the 'exclusive
responsibility' of the parties to carry on the peace talks, whereas the guarantors
had the 'autonomous capacity' to make recommendations, suggestions,
exhortations, declarations and evaluations on the matter. The operation of this ad
hoc mechanism, established by the 1942 Protocol of Rio de Janeiro, contributed
decisively to ease the tensions between Ecuador and Peru, in the search for a
settlement of their border problem.

---

15.   Ibid. In the early 1970s, fact-finding was also employed by the OAS Mission of
Observation in Belize (in 1972, pursuant to an agreement between Guatemala and the
United Kingdom).
16.   H. Gros Espiell, 'La Paz entre El Salvador y Honduras', *Revista Internacional y Diplomática*,
Vol. 30, 1981, n. 361, pp. 28–9.

There are other examples from the past.[17] Parallel to this trend of finding ad hoc solutions, there has been in the Latin American region a constant search for practical and flexible methods of peaceful settlement. This attitude also has historical roots, as illustrated by the old Inter-American Commission of Peace, created by the Meeting of Ministers of External Relations in Havana (1940) and formally constituted in 1948, and which, curiously, was to coexist with the procedures of the Bogotá Pact. Despite its non-conventional basis, it was successfully resorted to on various occasions, on account of its flexibility of action and agility (able to act *motu propio*).[18] The commission even had its powers extended in 1959, but it was later replaced, on the occasion of the 1967 reform of the OAS Charter (Protocol of Buenos Aires), by the Inter-American Commission on Peaceful Settlement, with wider powers but as a subsidiary organ of the OAS Permanent Council.[19]

However, the action of this new commission became conditioned by the requirement of prior consent of the contending parties. This accounted for a certain immobility on the part of the regional organization in the field of peaceful settlement from then onwards. Hence the continuing resort to ad hoc solutions, outside the institutional framework of the regional organization, with the resulting use of different methods of conflict resolution according to the circumstances of

17. In a more distant past, there were conflicts settled by inter-American procedures (such as the controversy between Haiti and the Dominican Republic in 1937, resolved by the Commission of Investigation and Conciliation established under the 1923 Treaty to Prevent Conflicts between American States (the so-called Gondra Treaty) and the 1929 Washington Convention of Inter-American Conciliation), as well as conflicts resolved not by mechanisms of existing treaties, but rather by ad hoc commissions (such as the frontier disputes between Guatemala and Honduras in 1930, and Peru and Ecuador in 1942, the Chaco conflict in 1929 and the Leticia controversy between Colombia and Peru in 1934 – the last two with the assistance of the League of Nations). A. A. Cançado Trindade, 'Os métodos de solução pacífica de controvérsias internacionais', *Estudos Jurídicos – Porto Alegre*, Vol. 17, 1984, n. 39, p. 110; see also pp. 89–126.
18. A. V. W. Thomas and A. J. Thomas Jr, *The Organization of American States*, pp. 125–8 and 301–2, Dallas, Southern Methodist University Press, 1963. Sepúlveda, op. cit., pp. 99–101 and 131. Fenwick, op. cit., pp. 198–208. A. Herrarte, 'Solución pacífica de las controversias en el sistema interamericano', *VI Curso de Derecho Internacional Organizado por el Comité Jurídico Interamericano (1979–1980)*, p. 231, OAS General Secretariat, 1980.
19. Sepúlveda, op. cit., pp. 129–30. Herrarte, op. cit., pp. 222–3.

each case.[20] It therefore becomes very difficult to generalize as to the effectiveness of each method of peaceful settlement.

For example, if direct negotiations proved successful between Argentina and Uruguay over the River Plate and its maritime front,[21] and between Brazil and Argentina over the use of waters of the River Paraná, and between the United States and Panama over the regime of the canal,[22] there are also cases in which the negotiations, extended over many years, have not produced entirely satisfactory results, such as the territorial problem between Venezuela and Guyana, and the controversy between Venezuela and Colombia as to maritime delimitation,[23] and the old issue between Bolivia and Chile concerning Bolivia's access to the sea.[24]

Methods of peaceful settlement other than direct negotiations have likewise been resorted to. In the controversy between Chile and Argentina over the Beagle Channel, for example, shortly after the arbitral award of 1977, the mediation of the Holy See (as from 1979) led to the 1984 treaty of peace between the two countries.[25] The resolution of the controversy over the Beagle Channel paved the way for the settlement of another boundary dispute between Argentina and Chile, over the Laguna del Desierto. This latter was submitted to an arbitral tribunal, which rendered its award on 21 October 1994 (followed by another award – on Chile's requests for revision and interpretation – of 13 October 1995).[26]

---

20. See, generally, A. A. Cançado Trindade, *O direito internacional e a solução pacífica das controvérsias internacionais*, pp. 3–135, Rio de Janeiro, SBERJ, 1988.

21. On the negotiations, see H. Gros Espiell, 'Le traité relatif au "Rio de la Plata" et sa façade maritime', *Annuaire français de droit international*, Vol. 21, 1975, pp. 241–9.

22. See, for example, R. Y. Chuang, 'The Process and Politics of the Ratification of the Panama Canal Treaties in the United States', *Revue de droit international de sciences diplomatiques et politiques*, Vol. 56, 1978, pp. 95–113.

23. For comments on this latter, see P. Gilhodes, 'Le conflit entre la Colombie et le Venezuela: quelques arpents d'eau salée?', *Revue française de science politique*, Vol. 21, 1971, pp. 1272–89.

24. See, for example, G. Echeverría, M. T. Infante and W. Sánchez, 'Chile y Bolivia: conflicto y negociación en la subregión', *Las relaciones entre los países de América Latina*, pp. 153–83, Santiago, Ed. Universitaria, 1980.

25. On the arbitral award, see, for example, J. Dutheil de la Rochère, 'L'affaire du Canal de Beagle', *Annuaire français de droit international*, Vol. 23, 1977, pp. 408–35.

26. For comments, see F. O. Salvioli, 'Las sentencias del tribunal arbitral sobre el diferendo argentino-chileno en relación al recorrido del límite entre el Hito 62 y el Monte Fiz Roy', *Boletim da Sociedade Brasileira de Direito Internacional*, Vol. 101/3, 1996, pp. 187–205.

Given this most diversified framework of resort to means of conflict resolution, most of them outside the institutional machinery of the regional organization, it was not surprising to find that, already in its first period of sessions in 1971, the OAS General Assembly had displayed some concern about the need to strengthen the inter-American system of peace.[27] Two years later, in 1973, the Special Commission to Study the Inter-American System and to Propose Measures for Its Restructuring (CEESI) dwelt upon the theme of the enhancement of the regional system of peaceful settlement.[28] Over a decade later, in an opinion of 1985, the Inter-American Juridical Committee went as far as proposing concrete changes in some of the provisions of the Bogotá Pact.[29]

The field of peaceful settlement of disputes became in fact an object of special attention of the second reform of the OAS Charter – that of the Protocol of Cartagena de Indias of 1985. Attentive to the reality of the matter in the region, endeavours focused on the search for individual solutions, adequate to each case. This implied an acknowledgement of the virtual immobility of the regional organization to take effective action in this field as from the first reform of its charter in 1967 (Protocol of Buenos Aires). This prompted the 1985 reform to devise more flexible methods of operation in conflict resolution.

Accordingly, the OAS Charter as amended by the 1985 Protocol of Cartagena was to authorize any party to a dispute – in relation to which none of the procedures foreseen in the charter was being used – to resort to the OAS Permanent Council to obtain its good offices (Article 84). Such unilateral recourse replaced the previous requirement of prior consent of both, or all, contending parties. Moreover, the former Inter-American Commission on Peaceful Settlement, set up by the 1967 reform of the OAS Charter (see above), was replaced by the OAS Permanent Council's new faculty of

---

27. *Comité Jurídico Interamericano, recomendaciones e informes – documentos oficiales 1967–1973*, Vol. 10, pp. 347–8 and 356, OAS General Secretariat, 1978.

28. OAS, document OEA/Ser.G/CP/CAJP-541/84, of 30 July 1984, pp. 88–9.

29. *Inter-American Juridical Committee, Recommendations and Reports 1985*, Vol. 17, pp. 57–94, OAS General Secretariat, 1987; see also account in Isidoro Zanotti, '[Report:] Regional and International Activities', *University of Miami Inter-American Law Review*, Vol. 17, 1986, pp. 339–44.

establishing ad hoc commissions, with the acquiescence of the contending parties (Articles 85–87).

A much more practical and flexible mechanism was thus devised, carefully avoiding, at the same time, 'imposing solutions' upon either of the parties.[30] Furthermore, the OAS Secretary-General became endowed with the new faculty or initiative of bringing to the attention of the OAS General Assembly or Permanent Council any question which in his opinion might affect peace on the continent (Article 116). While these initiatives of institutional reform of the OAS methods of action were being taken, with the apparent understanding that it would be proper and convenient to leave open to contending parties the best possibilities or schemes of peaceful settlement, once again it was outside the regional organization that means were pursued to tackle a grave situation that was indeed affecting peace on the continent: the Central American crisis.

Given the intensification of tension in the Central American region, coupled with the incapacity of international organizations to resolve the conflict, the foreign ministers of Panama, Mexico, Venezuela and Colombia convened a meeting on the Island of Contadora in January 1983 to formulate a proposal of dialogue and negotiation to reduce tension and re-establish peaceful coexistence between Central American states. The ensuing document was called the Declaration of Contadora (of 9 January 1983), and the four countries came to be known as the Group of Contadora.

Following initial efforts of good offices on the part of the presidents of the four countries, in June 1984 the foreign ministers of the Group of Contadora drew up a document (the so-called Act of Contadora)[31] containing the matters and recommendations agreed upon. In September of the same year, the Group of Contadora forwarded to the heads of state of the Central American countries a revised version of the Act of Contadora,[32] stressing the need to re-establish peace

---

30.   It was pointed out that the new mechanism in a way resembled the old Inter-American Commission of Peace (see above). Cf. F. Orrego Vicuña, 'La Búsqueda de un nuevo papel para la Organización de los Estados Americanos: El protocolo de reformas de la Carta de 1985', *Estudios Internacionales* (Santiago), Vol. 20, 1987, n. 77, pp. 73–5.

31.   Its full title was 'Act of Contadora for Peace and Co-operation in Central America'.

32.   Accompanied by four additional protocols.

in the region on the basis of compliance with the principles of international law and to undertake a joint search for a regional solution to the Central American crisis. Furthermore, it described the instruments of verification and inspection foreseen for the execution and follow-up of the commitments (*compromisos*) agreed upon.[33]

There remained major difficulties: the reduction of armaments and demilitarization, the operation of mechanisms of verification and control, and internal reconciliation. However, the negotiations pursued – together with consultations, ad hoc fact-finding mechanisms and good offices – and the international support they received, avoided the aggravation of the conflict with unforeseeable consequences not only for the region but for the whole continent. In mid-1985, the foreign ministers of Argentina, Brazil, Peru and Uruguay held informal consultations which led to the creation of the Group of Support to Contadora.

The two groups had their first joint meeting in Cartagena in August 1985. In the following months, with the frequency of meetings of the chancellors of the Groups of Contadora and of Support, the distinction between the two groups was gradually minimized and common operational initiatives were foreseen.[34] This was the historical meeting that led to the establishment later on of the Group of Rio, parallel to the OAS and with a much-expanded agenda, no longer centred on the Central American crisis.

Support to the Contadora process came at last from the presidents of the five Central American countries themselves (Guatemala, El Salvador, Honduras, Nicaragua and Costa Rica), in the declaration they adopted during their meeting in Esquipulas, Guatemala, on 25 May 1986 (Esquipulas I). It was followed by the Plan Arias, adopted by the five presidents in San José, Costa Rica, on 15 February 1987. On 6/7 August 1987 they met again in Esquipulas, where they at last agreed on and signed the Procedure for the Establishment of the Firm and Lasting Peace in Central America (Esquipulas II). The main commitments were directed

---

33. For a study, see A. A. Cançado Trindade, 'Mécanismes de règlement pacifique des différends en Amérique Centrale: de Contadora à Esquipulas-II', *Annuaire français de droit international*, Vol. 33, 1987, pp. 798–822.

34. For an account, see ibid.

towards national reconciliation, cease-fire, democratization and free elections, cessation of aid to irregular forces and rebels, non-use of territory to attack other states, assistance to refugees and displaced persons, and consolidation of democracy.[35] Two supervisory organs were promptly set up, namely, the International Commission of Verification and Follow-up and the Executive Committee.[36]

The procedure worked out in August 1987 saved time and occupied political space in the negotiating and fact-finding process. This finally resulted in a new atmosphere of peace in the Central American region. The Contadora/Esquipulas II process, as a whole, had the merit of avoiding an escalation of the regional conflict into one of much greater proportions and unforeseeable consequences for the whole continent.[37] This process, as already pointed out, evolved outside the institutional framework of the OAS and the United Nations, but eventually received the support of both organizations[38] (and of virtually the whole international community).

The process – even before Esquipulas I and II – was soon recognized as the only viable way to a negotiated peace in the region. Ultimately, it amounted to a non-institutionalized regional Latin American initiative to settle the Central American crisis on the basis of consensus of all parties concerned. Negotiations and fact-finding played a very important role in the settlement. The importance given to the international legal tradition of Latin American countries was another element of relevance in the successive formulae negotiated, which proved conducive to peace in the region.

However, there have been some cases involving two or more American states, that transcended the ambit of regional arrangements and were transferred to settlement at global (United Nations) level. An example is the Cuban missile crisis (1961), which went before the United Nations Security Council. There have

---

35. Points 7, 10 and 11 of Esquipulas II were of particular importance to the means of peaceful settlement.
36. For details, see Cançado Trindade, op. cit., pp. 798–822.
37. For a recent reassessment, see Jaime Ordóñez and Nuria Gamboa (eds.), *Esquipulas, diez años después: Hacia dónde va Centroamérica?*, pp. 1–30, San José, CSUCA, 1997.
38. Cançado Trindade, op. cit., pp. 798–822, especially p. 810, n. 57.

likewise been cases, channeled to judicial settlement, which ultimately were taken up by the International Court of Justice (ICJ). One may recall, in this connection, the asylum case between Colombia and Peru (1950/51),[39] the frontier conflict between Honduras and Nicaragua concerning the 1906 arbitral award of the King of Spain (1960),[40] the case of Nicaragua versus the United States,[41] and the case concerning the land, island and maritime frontier dispute between El Salvador and Honduras, with Nicaragua intervening.[42]

RESOLUTION OF OTHER TYPES OF DISPUTE

The judicial solution has also been resorted to in the settlement of disputes of a distinct character (individuals or private parties versus states) in two specific contexts, namely, that of subregional economic integration and that of the international protection of individual rights. As for the former, the Andean Pact, created by the 1969 Agreement of Cartagena (later extended by the 1988 Protocol of Quito), counts on a Court of Justice (*Tribunal de Justicia*), based in Quito, to secure respect for the interpretation and application of community law. The institutional framework pursued by the Andean Group was inspired by the example of the then European Communities (EEC), endowed likewise with a Court of Justice, based in Luxembourg.

The Andean Court of Justice, like its counterpart in the European Union, articulates with national courts and judges the proper application of community law by means of preliminary rulings. Furthermore, it sanctions breaches of community law by means of the so-called *acción de incumplimiento*. The nullity of

---

39. *ICJ Reports,* 1950, pp. 266–89; *ICJ Reports,* 1951, pp. 71–84.

40. *ICJ Reports,* 1960, pp. 192–217. The Bogotá Pact had in fact been invoked in the frontier conflict between Honduras and Nicaragua in 1957, and the recourse to the ICJ was made in the light of the pertinent provisions of the pact. See Lupinacci, op. cit., pp. 205–06; Thomas and Thomas Jr, op. cit., pp. 315–16.

41. *ICJ Reports,* 1984, pp. 392–443; *ICJ Reports,* 1986, pp. 14–150. For a case study, see Cançado Trindade, 'Nicarágua versus Estados Unidos: Os limites da jurisdição "obrigatória" da Corte Internacional de Justiça e as perspectivas da solução judicial de controvérsias internacionais', *Revista Brasileira de Estudos Políticos,* Vol. 31, 1987, pp. 139–70.

42. *ICJ Reports,* 1992, pp. 353–618.

those breaches – in case of *détournement de pouvoir* of decisions of the commission and the junta as community organs – can be the object of a suit open to both states parties and individuals or juridical persons. The first sentences of nullity of this kind were rendered by the Andean Court of Justice in June 1987.[43] The court's procedures were conceived, however, to secure respect for community law rather than to guarantee subjective rights, and a further restriction in this regard is found in the fact that the court cannot start operating *ex officio,* by its own initiative.[44]

The Common Market of the Southern Cone (Mercosul/Mercosur), created by the Treaty of Asunción of March 1991, has likewise, from the start, foreseen the establishment of a transitional system of settlement of controversies, as a first step towards the creation of a permanent system.[45] By the end of 1994, however, the states parties (Argentina, Brazil, Paraguay and Uruguay) deemed that the time had not yet come for the establishment of a permanent system of settlement of controversies in the ambit of Mercosul/Mercosur, and postponed it until the culmination of the process of convergence of a common external tariff. In the meantime, the transitional system – set forth in the Protocol of Brasilia of December 1991 and the Protocol of Ouro Preto of December 1994 – applies.[46]

Under the current system, controversies between the states parties on the interpretation and application of the *corpus juris* of the Common Market of the Southern Cone are to be settled, first, through negotiations. If these do not succeed, the complaint by the state concerned can be lodged with the Commission of Commerce of Mercosul/Mercosur. If consensus is not reached therein, the

---

43. See, for example: L. C. Sáchica, *Derecho Comunitario Andino*, 2nd. ed., pp. 97–126, Bogotá, Temis, 1990; G. Larenas, *El Tribunal de Justicia Andino*, pp. 11–37, Quito, CCE, 1980; G. Moreno Loayza, *El Tribunal de Justicia del Acuerdo de Cartagena como medio jurídico de solución de controversias*, pp. 109–203, Quito, TJAC, 1987; J. G. Andueza, *El Tribunal del Pacto Andino*, pp. 81–160, Quito, TJAC, 1986.
44. Sáchica, op. cit., pp. 104–15.
45. Article 3 and Annex III of the 1991 Treaty of Asunción.
46. For a study, see, for example, E. Grebler, 'A Solução de Controvérsias no Tratado do Mercosul', in P. B. Casella (ed.), *Contratos Internacionais e Direito Econômico no Mercosul*, pp. 348–62, São Paulo, Ed. LTr, 1996. V. Marotta Rangel, 'Solução de Controvérsias após Ouro Preto', in ibid., pp. 692–701.

154 Antonio Augusto Cançado Trindade

complaint is taken to the Group Common Market. In case of non-compliance with the latter's decision, the arbitral procedure comes into operation. This is the last stage of the conflict resolution, not only as regards interstate disputes, but also in respect of complaints from individuals and juridical persons, channelled through the states concerned.

The arbitral procedure is limited, however, to the institution of ad hoc tribunals, to be based in Asunción. This transitional system, as it now stands, appears hardly satisfactory for a scheme of subregional integration such as that of Mercosul/Mercosur. As ad hoc tribunals are by definition bound to be rather episodic and discontinued, states parties are likely to feel the need in the future to endow the Mercosul/Mercosur regime with a permanent judicial organ of the same kind as the Courts of Justice of the Andean Pact and the European Union, capable of securing the uniform interpretation and application of the norms of community law.[47]

As for the general protection of individual rights *vis-à-vis* the state, a pioneering experiment on the American continent was that of the establishment in 1907 of the Central American Court of Justice, which received and examined cases lodged with it by individuals against the states parties. Although the experiment came to an end after ten years, in 1917, with the expiry of the non-renewed treaty that created it, the court – which preceded even the old Permanent Court of International Justice – is nowadays regarded as the first permanent international tribunal of modern times.[48] It may have been too advanced an experiment for its time.

The protection of individual rights – by means of the contraposition of individual claimants to respondent states – was, however, to undergo considerable evolution over the last fifty years in the domain of the international protection of

---

47. See, in this sense, Grebler, op. cit., pp. 361–2. Marotta Rangel, op. cit., p. 701.
48. For a study, see C. J. Gutiérrez, *La Corte de Justicia Centroamericana*, 3rd. ed., pp. 24–158, San José, Juricentro, 1978; A. A. Cançado Trindade, 'Exhaustion of Local Remedies in International Law Experiments Granting Procedural Status to Individuals in the First Half of the Twentieth Century', *Netherlands International Law Review*, Vol. 24, 1977, pp. 373–92; M. O. Hudson, 'The Central American Court of Justice', *American Journal of International Law*, 1932, pp. 774–85.

human rights. As far as the American continent is concerned, the two supervisory organs of the 1969 American Convention on Human Rights (in force since mid-1978) – the Inter-American Commission and Court of Human Rights – have received and examined individual complaints or communications on alleged human-rights violations. Those complaints are first lodged with the commission, and have to comply with the conditions of admissibility set forth in the Convention (Articles 46–47). The commission may either adopt a final report on a case or refer it to the court (Article 51).

By the early 1990s, the commission had decided on more than 15,000 individual complaints. It has over 800 communications pending. The court, in its turn, has heard or admitted twenty-seven contentious cases and has delivered fifty judgements (relating to preliminary objections, merits, reparations, and interpretation of judgements). Moreover, it has so far delivered fifteen advisory opinions.[49]

Due to the endeavours of the Inter-American Court and Commission, many lives have been saved, reparations have been granted, legislative measures have been adopted or modified, wrongful administrative practices have been terminated, positive measures and educational programmes have been adopted. But the two supervisory organs still confront problems today, generated largely by the persistence of human-rights violations in different parts of the region, by new and diversified forms of those violations (requiring greater flexibility), and the insufficiency of human and material resources to undertake their work efficiently.[50]

A brief reference could also be made to recent developments in international refugee law in Latin America. The 1984 Cartagena Declaration on Refugees gave a wider dimension to the protection of refugees in the region by focusing the

49. All figures as of 14 June 1999.
50. For an assessment, see A. A. Cançado Trindade, 'El sistema interamericano de protección de los derechos humanos (1948–1995): Evolución, estado actual y perspectivas', *Derecho internacional y derechos humanos/Droit international et droits de l'homme (Libro Conmemorativo de la XXIV Sesión del Programa Exterior de la Academia de Derecho Internacional de La Haya, San José de Costa Rica, Abril/Mayo 1995)*, pp. 47–95, The Hague/San José, IIDH/Académie de Droit International de La Haye, 1996.

matter in the conceptual universe of human rights. One decade later, the 1994 San José Declaration on Refugees and Displaced Persons went deeper into the interrelation between the law on refugees and displaced persons and human-rights law. Those two regional instruments, though declaratory in nature, have succeeded in extending protection to a much-increased number of persons in great need of it.[51]

FINAL REMARKS

Apart from the settlement of such distinct types of dispute, which takes place on a permanent basis in very specific contexts and within clearly defined parameters of international treaties and instruments, it is to the resolution of interstate conflicts in the Latin American region that we shall devote these final remarks. Latin America is a region with a long-standing and rich tradition of public international law in general, and in interstate conflict resolution in particular. The multiplicity of procedures adopted to this end, over the years, should, however, be approached in a critical spirit, as it might well be symptomatic of their own insufficiencies.

Parallel to the constant and unsuccessful endeavours to secure some degree of effectiveness to the comprehensive codifying treaty on peaceful settlement of disputes in the region (the 1948 Bogotá Pact), a rich practice developed of conflict resolution on an ad hoc basis, seeking individual solutions to each case. This practice has in some cases produced concrete positive results with the achievement of peace. This has taken place in most instances outside the institutional mechanisms of the regional system of peace. A variety of means of settlement have been resorted to, ranging from negotiations and consultations to good offices and conciliation, from fact-finding to mediation, as well as arbitration and the judicial solution.

---

51. For an assessment, see IIDH/ACNUR, *10 Años de la Declaración de Cartagena sobre Refugiados – Memoria del Coloquio Internacional (San José de Costa Rica, Diciembre 1994)*, pp. 11–470, San José, IIDH/ACNUR/Costa Rican Government, 1995.

By and large, states have in most cases displayed a certain preference for less rigid and more flexible methods of conflict resolution, suitable to the circumstances. But this has not prevented them from resorting, in a few cases, to arbitral and judicial solutions. It is therefore very difficult to generalize as to the effectiveness of a given method of peaceful settlement. The pattern of diversity of means of conflict resolution and of the search for individual solutions is, besides being clearly identifiable, a reflection of the perennial tension between states' general duty of peaceful settlement and their freedom of choice or the means of settlement. Such ambivalence has always permeated public international law relating to conflict resolution.

In international adjudication, for example, the so-called 'compulsory jurisdiction' of international organs remains to date a *vexata quaestio,* illustrating the regrettable lack of automatism in international jurisdiction. This being so, the behaviour of contending states – not only in Latin America but in all parts of the world – has always attempted to condition the means of settlement (selecting whatever appears most favourable to them) as well as the very configuration of the dispute at issue (insisting on their own version of the facts). This adds an element of unpredictability to conflict resolution.

Thus, settlement of disputes remains a domain of international law and relations, strongly impregnated with state voluntarism, despite all recent attempts at codification and progressive development on a global level.[52] It has so far yielded to the voluntarist conception of international law, which prevailed in the past but is today under heavy criticism. In fact, if states create and apply norms of international law by their own free will, as that doctrine sustains, it is also by their

---

52. Such as, for example, at the United Nations level, the 1982 Manila Declaration on the Peaceful Settlement of International Disputes; the 1988 United Nations Declaration on the Prevention and Removal of Disputes and Situations Which May Threaten International Peace and Security and on the Role of the United Nations on This Field; and various United Nations General Assembly resolutions (including resolution 44/21 of 15/11/1989) on the enhancement of international peace in accordance with the United Nations Charter. See Boutros-Ghali, op. cit., 2nd. ed. (suppl.), p. 52, New York, United Nations, 1995. See also *United Nations, Handbook on the Peaceful Settlement of Disputes between States,* pp. 1–153, New York, United Nations, 1992.

free will that they violate those norms, and the voluntarist conception thus revolves in a vicious circle that can hardly provide a reasonable explanation for the evolution of general international law.[53]

Other domains of public international law have long overcome the voluntarist dogma (for example, the international protection of human rights, the law of international organizations, the international regulation of spaces – particularly as regards the so-called 'global commons' – the international protection of the environment), and there is reason to hope that conflict resolution may some day also evolve to that end. There exists, nowadays at least, a growing awareness of factors that can pave the way to advances in the future. First, there is consensus today on the importance of prevention – of taking all possible preventive measures to avoid the outbreak and escalation of conflicts. Second, the understanding now prevails that the resolution of conflicts must not only focus on the symptoms alone, but should also encompass the underlying causes that generate them[54] and their removal, if a durable solution is ever to be achieved. Last but not least, there is today a generalized awareness of the need to find permanent solutions to conflicts, and of the virtual impossibility of reaching them without applying fairness and justice. Peace and justice go hand in hand and one cannot be achieved without the other.

BIBLIOGRAPHICAL REFERENCES

Books

ANDUEZA, J. G. *El Tribunal del Pacto Andino*, Quito, TJAC, 1986.

BOUTROS-GHALI, B. *An Agenda for Peace*. 2nd. ed. + supp., New York, United Nations, 1995.

---

53. A. A. Cançado Trindade, 'The Voluntarist Conception of International Law: A Reassessment', *Revue de droit international de sciences diplomatiques et politiques*, Vol. 59, 1981, pp. 201–40, esp. pp. 224–5.
54. Boutros-Ghali, op. cit., pp. 5–72, esp. p. 37.

CANÇADO TRINDADE, A. A. *O direito internacional e a solução pacífica das controvérsias internacionais*, Rio de Janeiro, SBERJ, 1988.

FENWICK, C. G. *The Organization of American States.* Washington, D.C., Kaufmann Pr., 1963.

GUTIÉRREZ, C. J. *La Corte de Justicia Centroamericana.* 3rd. ed. San José, Juricentro, 1978.

IIDH/ACNUR, *10 Años de la Declaración de Cartagena sobre Refugiados – Memoria del Coloquio Internacional* (San José, Costa Rica, December 1994). San José, IIDH/ACNUR/Costa Rican Government, 1995.

LARENAS, G. *El Tribunal de Justicia Andino.* Quito, CCE, 1980.

MORENO LOAYZA, G. *El Tribunal de Justicia del Acuerdo de Cartagena como medio jurídico de solución de controversias.* Quito, TJAC, 1987.

ORDOÑEZ, J.; GAMBOA, N. (eds.). *Esquipulas, diez años después: hacia dónde va Centroamérica?* San José, CSUCA, 1997.

SACHICA, L. C. *Derecho comunitario andino*, 2nd. ed. Bogotá, Temis, 1990.

THOMAS, A. V. W.; THOMAS Jr., A. J. *The Organization of American States.* Dallas, Southern Methodist University Press, 1963.

UNITED NATIONS. *Handbook on the Peaceful Settlement of Disputes between States.* New York, United Nations, 1992.

Articles

BRIGGS, H. W. The Optional Protocols of Geneva (1958) and Vienna (1961, 1963) Concerning the Compulsory Settlement of Disputes. *Recueil d'études de droit international en hommage à Paul Guggenheim* (Geneva, IUHEI), 1968, pp. 628–41.

CAICEDO CASTILLA, J. J. El Arbitraje en las Conferencias Panamericanas hasta el Pacto de Bogotá de 1948 sobre Soluciones Pacíficas. *Boletim da Sociedade Brasileira de Direito Internacional,* Vol. 4, 1948, pp. 5–33.

CANÇADO TRINDADE, A. A. El sistema interamericano de protección de los derechos humanos (1948–1995): evolución, estado actual y perspectivas'. *Derecho internacional y derechos humanos/Droit international et droits de l'homme (Libro Conmemorativo de la XXIV Sesión del Programa Exterior de la Academia de Derecho Internacional de La Haya, San José de Costa Rica, Abril/Mayo 1995),* The Hague/San José, IIDH/Académie de Droit International de La Haye, 1996, pp. 47–95.

—. Exhaustion of Local Remedies in International Law Experiments Granting Procedural Status to Individuals in the First Half of the Twentieth Century. *Netherlands International Law Review*, Vol. 24, 1977, pp. 373–92.

—. Mécanismes de règlement pacifique des différends en Amérique Centrale: de Contadora à Esquipulas II'. *Annuaire français de droit international*, Vol. 33, 1987, pp. 798–822.

—. Nicarágua versus Estados Unidos: Os limites da jurisdição 'obrigatória' da Corte Internacional de Justiça e as perspectivas da solução judicial de controvérsias internacionais. *Revista Brasileira de Estudos Políticos*, Vol. 31, 1987, pp. 139–70.

—. Os métodos de solução pacífica de controvérsias internacionais'. *Estudos Jurídicos* (Porto Alegre), Vol. 17, No. 39, 1984, pp. 89–126.

—. The Voluntarist Conception of International Law: A Reassessment. *Revue de droit international de sciences diplomatiques et politiques*, Vol. 59, 1981, pp. 201–40.

CHUANG, R. Y. The Process and Politics of the Ratification of the Panama Canal Treaties in the United States. *Revue de droit international de sciences diplomatiques et politiques*, Vol. 56, 1978, pp. 95–113.

DUPUY, R. J. Codification et règlement des différends – Les débats de Vienne sur les procédures de règlement. *Annuaire français de droit international*, Vol. 15, 1969, pp. 70–90.

DUTHEIL DE LA ROCHERE, J. L'affaire du Canal de Beagle. *Annuaire français de droit international*, Vol. 23, 1977, pp. 408–35.

ECHEVERRIA, G.; INFANTE, M. T.; SANCHEZ, W. Chile y Bolivia: Conflicto y negociación en la subregión. In: W. Sánchez (ed.), *Las relaciones entre los países de América Latina*, pp. 153–83, Santiago, Ed. Universitaria, 1980.

GILHODES, P. Le conflit entre la Colombie et le Venezuela: quelques arpents d'eau salée? *Revue française de science politique*, Vol. 21, 1971, pp. 1272–89.

GREBLER, E. A Solução de Controvérsias no Tratado do Mercosul. In: P. B. Casella (ed.), *Contratos internacionais e direito econômico no Mercosul*, pp. 348–62, São Paulo, Ed. LTr, 1996.

GROS ESPIELL, H. La Paz entre El Salvador y Honduras. *Revista Internacional y Diplomática*, Vol. 30, No. 361, 1981, pp. 28–9.

—. Le traité relatif au 'Rio de la Plata' et sa façade maritime. *Annuaire français de droit international*, Vol. 21, 1975, pp. 241–9.

HERRARTE, A. Solución pacífica de las controversias en el sistema interamericano, *VI Curso de Derecho Internacional Organizado por el Comité Jurídico Interamericano (1979–1980)* (OAS General Secretariat), p. 231.

HUDSON, M. O. The Central American Court of Justice. *American Journal of International Law*, 1932, pp. 774–85.

LAGOS, E. Los nuevos mecanismos procesales para la eficacia de la solución pacífica de las controversias, con particular referencia a la práctica de la OEA en los últimos años. *Perspectivas del Derecho Internacional Contemporáneo*, Vol. 2 (Santiago, Universidad de Chile), 1981, pp. 79–91.

LUPINACCI, J. C. Los procedimientos jurisdiccionales en el tratado americano de soluciones pacíficas (Pacto de Bogotá). *Anuario Uruguayo de Derecho Internacional*, 1962, pp. 205–6.

MAROTTA RANGEL, V. Solução de controvérsias após Ouro Preto. In: P. B. Casella (ed.), *Contratos internacionais e direito econômico no Mercosul*, pp. 692–701, São Paulo, Ed. LTr, 1996.

ORREGO VICUÑA, F. Análisis de la práctica latinoamericana en materia de solución de controversias durante la década de 1970 y sus implicaciones para el futuro. *Perspectivas del derecho internacional.*

—. La Búsqueda de un nuevo papel para la Organización de los Estados Americanos: El protocolo de reformas de la carta de 1985. *Estudios Internacionales – Santiago*, Vol. 20, No. 77, 1987, pp. 73–5.

ROSENNE, S. The Settlement of Treaty Disputes under the Vienna Convention of 1969. *Zeitschrift für ausländisches öffentliches Recht und Völkerrecht*, Vol. 31, 1971, pp. 1–62.

SALVIOLI, F. O. Las sentencias del tribunal arbitral sobre el diferendo argentino-chileno en relación al recorrido del límite entre el hito 62 y el Monte Fiz Roy. *Boletim da Sociedade Brasileira de Direito Internacional*. Vol. 101/103, 1996, pp. 187–205.

SEPULVEDA, C. The Reform of the Charter of the Organization of American States. *Recueil des Cours de l'Académie de Droit International*, Vol. 137, 1972, pp. 107–8.

YEPES, J. M., La Conférence Panaméricaine de Bogotá et le droit international américain. *Revue générale de droit international public,* 1949, pp. 52–74.

ZANOTTI, I. Regional and International Activities (Report). *University of Miami Inter-American Law Review,* Vol. 17, 1986, pp. 339–44.

About the authors

Mohammed BEDJAOUI
Member of the International Court of Justice; President of the Court from 1994 to 1997

Yves DAUDET
Professor of international relations and Vice-president of the University of Paris I-Panthéon-Sorbonne

Takashi INOGUCHI
Professor of political science, University of Tokyo's Institute of Oriental Culture

Rudolf JOO
Deputy State Secretary of the Ministry of Foreign Affairs, Hungary

Wojciech MULTAN
Professor of international relations, Gdansk University, Poland

Reka SZRMERKENYI
Adviser to the Prime Minister for International Affairs, Hungary

Emmanuel ROUCOUNAS
Professor of international law, Athens University, Greece; Member of the
Institute of International Law

Antonio A. Cançado TRINDADE
President of the Inter-American Court of Human Rights;
Executive Director of the Inter-American Institute of Human Rights (1994–96)

Advisory Board for UNESCO's series on Peace and Conflict Issues

Vasu GOUNDEN
Director
African Centre for the Constructive Resolution of Disputes
c/o University of Durban Westville
Private Bag X54001
Durban 4000
South Africa

Fèlix MARTI
Director
Centre UNESCO de Catalunya
Mallorca, 285
08037 Barcelona
Spain

Sanaa W. OSSEIRAN
Vice-president
International Peace Research Association (IPRA)
Farah Building, Makhoul Street
Ras-Beirut
Beirut
Lebanon

Adam Daniel ROTFELD
Director
Stockholm International Peace Research Institute (SIPRI)
Frösunda
S-171 53 Solna
Sweden

Yoshikasu SAKAMOTO
Deputy Director
International Peace Research Institute Meigaku (PRIME)
1518 Kamikurata
Totsukaku-Yokohama 144
Japan

Dan SMITH
Director
International Peace Research Institute (PRIO)
Fuglenauggata, 11
N-0260 Oslo 2
Norway

Juan SOMAVIA
Director-General
International Labour Office
4, route des Morillons
1211 Geneva 22
Switzerland

Janusz SYMONIDES
Director
Department for Peace, Human Rights, Democracy and Tolerance
UNESCO

Anatoly TORKOUNOV
Rector
Moscow State Institute of International Relations
Foreign Affairs Ministry of the Russian Federation
76 Vernadskovo Avenue
117854 Moscow
Russian Federation

Lev VORONKOV
Director
International Institute for Peace
Möllwaldplatz 5
A-1040 Vienna
Austria